BANKING AND BANKING DEVELOPMENTS

SAFETY AND SOUNDNESS OF U.S. BANKS

ISSUES AND POLICIES IN BRIEF

BANKING AND BANKING DEVELOPMENTS

Additional books in this series can be found on Nova's website under the Series tab.

Additional E-books in this series can be found on Nova's website under the E-book tab.

BANKING AND BANKING DEVELOPMENTS

SAFETY AND SOUNDNESS OF U.S. BANKS

ISSUES AND POLICIES IN BRIEF

STEVEN B. KING

AND

BRIAN L. CARTER

EDITORS

New York

For permission to use material from this book please contact us:
Telephone 631-231-7269; Fax 631-231-8175
Web Site: http://www.novapublishers.com

Additional color graphics may be available in the e-book version of this book.

LIBRARY OF CONGRESS CATALOGING-IN-PUBLICATION DATA

ISBN: 978-1-62618-904-1

Published by Nova Science Publishers, Inc. † New York

CONTENTS

Preface		**vii**
Chapter 1	Financial Condition of Depository Banks *Darryl E. Getter*	**1**
Chapter 2	U.S. Implementation of the Basel Capital Regulatory Framework *Darryl E. Getter*	**21**
Chapter 3	Federal Deposit Insurance for Banks and Credit Unions *Darryl E. Getter*	**49**
Index		**79**

PREFACE

Congressional interest in the financial conditions of depository banks or the commercial banking industry has increased in the wake of the financial crisis that unfolded in 2007-2009, which resulted in a large increase in the number of distressed institutions. A financially strained banking system would have difficulty making credit available to facilitate macroeconomic recovery. This book focuses on the financial condition of the banking industry, which can be examined in terms of profitability, lending activity, and capitalization levels.

Chapter 1 – A bank is an institution that obtains either a federal or state charter that allows it to accept federally insured deposits and pay interest to depositors. In addition, the charter allows banks to make residential and commercial mortgage loans; provide check cashing and clearing services; underwrite securities that include U.S. Treasuries, municipal bonds, commercial paper, and Fannie Mae and Freddie Mac issuances; and other activities as defined by statute.

Congressional interest in the financial conditions of depository banks or the commercial banking industry has increased in the wake of the financial crisis that unfolded in 2007 2009, which resulted in a large increase in the number of distressed institutions. A financially strained banking system would have difficulty making credit available to facilitate macroeconomic recovery.

The financial condition of the banking industry can be examined in terms of profitability, lending activity, and capitalization levels (to buffer against the financial risks). This report focuses primarily on profitability and lending activity levels. Capitalization issues are discussed in *U.S. Implementation of the Basel Capital Regulatory Framework*, by Darryl E. Getter.

The metrics related to asset performance and earnings show an increase in profitability for the banking industry although many small bank institutions are still experiencing distress. Non- current loans still exceed the capacity of the banking industry to absorb potential losses if they were all to become uncollectible. Consequently, lending activities are likely to be restrained until bank loan-loss capacity as well as overall economic conditions improve. Furthermore, profitability in banking is not likely to indicate that pre-crisis lending patterns have resumed. Given the required increases in capitalization buffers to absorb loan defaults as well as the (expected) costs associated with funding loans, profitability trends may differ for banks by size, particularly after accounting for differences in the revenue generating activities of small and large banks.

Chapter 2 – The Basel III international regulatory framework, which was produced in 2010 by the Basel Committee on Banking Supervision at the Bank for International Settlements, is the latest in a series of evolving agreements among central banks and bank supervisory authorities to standardize bank capital requirements, among other measures. Capital serves as a cushion against sudden financial shocks (such as an unusually high occurrence of loan defaults), which can otherwise lead to insolvency. The Basel III regulatory reform package revises the definition of regulatory capital and increases capital holding requirements for banking organizations. The quantitative requirements and phase-in schedules for Basel III were approved by the 27-member jurisdictions and 44 central banks and supervisory authorities on September 12, 2010, and endorsed by the G20 leaders on November 12, 2010. Basel III recommends that banks satisfy these enhanced requirements by 2019. The Basel agreements are not treaties; individual countries can make modifications to suit their specific needs and priorities when implementing national bank capital requirements.

In the United States, Congress mandated enhanced bank capital requirements as part of financial- sector reform in the Dodd-Frank Wall Street Reform and Consumer Protection Act of 2010 (Dodd-Frank Act; P.L. 111-203, 124 Stat.1376). Specifically, the Collins Amendment to Dodd- Frank (1) amends the definition of capital; (2) establishes minimum capital and leverage requirements for banking subsidiaries, bank holding companies, and systemically important non- bank financial companies; and (3) establishes an implementation timeline shorter than that agreed to in the Basel III Accord. In addition, Dodd-Frank removes a requirement that credit ratings be referenced when evaluating the creditworthiness of financial securities. Instead, the Federal Banking Regulators (i.e., the Federal Reserve, the Office of the

Comptroller of the Currency, and the Federal Deposit Insurance Corporation) are required to find other appropriate standards by which to determine the financial risks of bank portfolio holdings when enforcing the mandatory capital requirements.

Chapter 3 – The federal deposit insurance system in the United States protects depositors from losses that would occur in the event that a financial institution becomes insolvent, meaning that the institution's lending activities did not generate enough revenue to repay depositors their principal and interest. By guaranteeing depositor accounts up to a set limit, deposit insurance may also help prevent "runs," which occur when bank customers lose confidence in the ability of a financial institution to repay its depositors and rush to withdraw deposits. A bank run, or panic, can spread and threaten the solvency of other financial institutions should the public also doubt their soundness, thus suddenly and simultaneously withdrawing deposits from those institutions as well. In other words, deposit insurance aims to promote and help maintain public confidence in the U.S. financial system, particularly at times when some depository entities suffer large losses or become insolvent.

The Federal Deposit Insurance Corporation (FDIC) was established to insure bank deposits as an independent government corporation under the authority of the Banking Act of 1933, also known as the Glass-Steagall Act (48 Stat. 162, 12 U.S.C.). The FDIC is not funded by appropriations; it is funded through insurance assessments collected from its member depository institutions and held in what is now known as the Deposit Insurance Fund (DIF). The proceeds in the DIF are used to pay depositors if member institutions fail.

The Federal Credit Union Act of 1934 (48 Stat. 1216) formed a national system to charter and supervise federal credit unions. The National Credit Union Administration (NCUA), which administers deposit insurance for credit unions, became an independent federal agency in 1970 (P.L. 91-468, 84 Stat. 994). The NCUA is not funded by appropriations, but through insurance assessments collected from its member credit union institutions and held in what is now known as the National Credit Union Share Insurance Fund (NCUSIF). Proceeds from the NCUSIF are used to pay share depositors if member institutions fail.

Beginning in 2008, the number of bank failures increased substantially, and the DIF fell below its statutory minimum requirement. Credit union failures also increased, and five large corporate credit unions were placed under conservatorship by the NCUA. The 111th Congress subsequently provided both the FDIC and the NCUA with greater ability to replenish the insurance funds and stabilize liquidity among depository institutions through a variety of measures. Should insurance claims (resulting from failures) exceed the sizes of the insurance fund reserves, additional legislative action may be necessary for one or both agencies to continue to resolve failed institutions.

Current congressional interest in deposit insurance relates to oversight of how the FDIC and the NCUA protect deposits and address solvency issues associated with their insurance funds. This report provides an overview of the FDIC and NCUA, the status of both the DIF and NCUSIF, and describes the procedures followed to resolve failed depository institutions. Appendixes to this report describe measures taken to reduce the loss exposure and total risks to the funds.

In: Safety and Soundness of U.S. Banks ISBN: 978-1-62618-904-1
Editors: S. B. King and B. L. Carter

Chapter 1

FINANCIAL CONDITION OF DEPOSITORY BANKS*

Darryl E. Getter

SUMMARY

A bank is an institution that obtains either a federal or state charter that allows it to accept federally insured deposits and pay interest to depositors. In addition, the charter allows banks to make residential and commercial mortgage loans; provide check cashing and clearing services; underwrite securities that include U.S. Treasuries, municipal bonds, commercial paper, and Fannie Mae and Freddie Mac issuances; and other activities as defined by statute.

Congressional interest in the financial conditions of depository banks or the commercial banking industry has increased in the wake of the financial crisis that unfolded in 2007-2009, which resulted in a large increase in the number of distressed institutions. A financially strained banking system would have difficulty making credit available to facilitate macroeconomic recovery.

The financial condition of the banking industry can be examined in terms of profitability, lending activity, and capitalization levels (to buffer against the financial risks). This report focuses primarily on profitability and lending

---

* This is an edited, reformatted and augmented version of the Congressional Research Service Publication, CRS Report for Congress R43002, dated March 18, 2013.

activity levels. Capitalization issues are discussed in *U.S. Implementation of the Basel Capital Regulatory Framework*, by Darryl E. Getter.

The metrics related to asset performance and earnings show an increase in profitability for the banking industry although many small bank institutions are still experiencing distress. Non- current loans still exceed the capacity of the banking industry to absorb potential losses if they were all to become uncollectible. Consequently, lending activities are likely to be restrained until bank loan-loss capacity as well as overall economic conditions improve. Furthermore, profitability in banking is not likely to indicate that pre-crisis lending patterns have resumed. Given the required increases in capitalization buffers to absorb loan defaults as well as the (expected) costs associated with funding loans, profitability trends may differ for banks by size, particularly after accounting for differences in the revenue generating activities of small and large banks.

INTRODUCTION

Financial intermediation is the process of matching savers, who are willing to lend funds to earn a future rate of return, with borrowers, who are presently in need of funds to make transactions. It is expensive, however, for savers to locate, underwrite, and monitor repayment behavior of borrowers. Similarly, it is expensive for borrowers to locate a sufficient amount of savers with funds and favorable lending terms. Hence, banks develop expertise in *intermediation*, or facilitating the transfer of funds from savers to borrowers. Although other institutions (e.g., credit unions, insurance companies, pension funds, hedge funds) also engage in the financial intermediation matching process, this report examines how depository banks are faring in this activity.

A commercial or depository bank is typically a corporation that obtains either a federal or state charter to accept federally insured deposits and pay interest to depositors; make residential and commercial mortgage loans; provide check cashing and clearing services; and may underwrite securities that include U.S. Treasuries, municipal bonds, Fannie Mae and Freddie Mac issuances, and commercial paper (unsecured short-term loans to cover short-term liquidity needs). The permissible activities of depository banks are defined by statute.[1]

The typical intermediation transaction made by banks consists of providing loans to borrowers at higher rates than the cost to borrow the funds from savers, who provide loanable funds in the form of bank deposits. Banks profit from the *spread* between the rates they receive from borrowers and the rates they pay to depositors. Facilitation of the intermediation transaction involves risk. Banks face the risk that borrowers can default on their loans, making it more difficult to repay depositors. In addition, banks face funding or liquidity risk stemming from more frequent movements in short-term interest rates. Banks must have access to an uninterrupted source of short-term funding (deposits) until its long-term loans are fully repaid, which is explained in more detail later in this report, and fluctuations in short rates translates into fluctuations in their profit spreads. Furthermore, depositors could suddenly and simultaneously decide to withdraw their deposits, perhaps due to a sudden change in economic conditions or even speculation about deteriorating economic conditions, resulting in financial distress for a bank or several banks.[2] Hence, bank profitability and financial risk are inextricably linked.

In addition to default and funding risks, financial intermediation increases the vulnerability of borrowers to economic downturns. During business cycle booms, lenders may grow optimistic and increase credit availability as if the ideal economic and financial market conditions will persist.[3] The trade-off or costs associated with an expansion of lending is a corresponding rise in the severity of financial distress should economic conditions suddenly deteriorate. In other words, recessions that occur when individuals have more loan repayment obligations (or more leveraged financially) are likely to be more arduous, in particular if these individuals (via job losses or pay cuts) suddenly face lower income prospects.

Hence, U.S. depository banks are required to comply with *safety and soundness* regulations, which are designed to monitor and buffer against the types of financial intermediation risks that can result in financial distress for banks and the broader economy. The propagation of intermediation risks is curbed when lending activity is restrained, but there is a cost associated with a reduction of financial risk. Recessions are likely to be milder when fewer loan repayment obligations are outstanding, but the trade-off is a less robust economic expansion. Fewer loans translate into fewer transactions that could possibly have spurred greater economic activity.[4] Consequently, determining how much financial intermediation risk is optimal for the banking system to take while simultaneously trying not to undermine economically stimulative lending activity is often a regulatory challenge.

Congressional interest in the financial conditions of depository banks, also referred to as the commercial banking system, has increased following an increase in distressed institutions and widespread credit tightening. The conditions of the banking industry can be examined in terms of profitability, lending activity, and capitalization levels (to buffer against the financial risks); but this report focuses primarily on profitability and lending activity levels. Particular attention will be paid to metrics related to asset performance and earnings of depository banks. These measures show that profitability for the banking industry has improved, but lending activity has not returned to pre-crisis levels.

IMPORTANT DEFINITIONS AND DISTRIBUTION BY SIZE

This report discusses the depository (commercial) banking institutions as having one aggregate balance sheet. The following balance sheet terminology is used.

- Bank *assets* include long-term consumer, residential, and commercial loans that banks originate as well as cash and other financial securities that they hold in their asset portfolios. Bank assets will generate earnings (revenues) or losses, depending upon whether customers repay or default on their loans.
- Bank *liabilities* include the funds that they borrow. When customers (depositors) make savings or checking deposits into a bank, the bank is essentially borrowing those funds for short periods of time in order to lend them out for longer periods of time. The interest paid for these borrowings are, therefore, the costs incurred by the bank to obtain the funds necessary to originate new loans.
- Bank *capital* is the difference between the value of assets and liabilities. Bank capital includes items such as common shareholder equity, retained earnings, and provisions set aside for loan and lease losses (discussed in more detail below). Banks that accept federally insured deposits are required to maintain sufficient capital reserves to protect bank creditors from loan defaults by bank customers. Asset (loan) defaults are less likely to result in failure of a bank to repay its shorter-term obligations if sufficient capital is maintained to absorb the losses. If, however, a bank's capital falls below minimum regulatory threshold levels, it would be considered undercapitalized and faces the prospect of being shut down by its regulator, which typically appoints the Federal Deposit Insurance Company (FDIC) [5] as the receiver of the insolvent institution. Consequently, compliance

with regulatory capital requirements implies that capital reserves must grow proportionately with bank asset (lending) portfolios.[6]

Assets in the banking industry are not evenly distributed, which means that banking firms are not identical and, for some metrics, must be analyzed separately to get a more accurate assessment of financial conditions. Using data from the FDIC, **Figure 1** illustrates the number of U.S. banks over time by the following size categories of bank asset holdings (defined below): less than $100 million, $100 million-$1 billion, $1 billion-$10 billion, and greater than $10 billion. Community banks are commonly defined as financial institutions with total assets below $1 billion.[7] At the other extreme are the large financial institutions that have $10 billion or more in assets. The number of banks with more than $10 billion in assets has remained relatively constant, ranging from 95 to 108 institutions over the period.

Figure 1 also shows the dollar amount of bank assets in millions of dollars. As of 2012, the FDIC reports that industry assets were $14,450.67 billion. For several decades, bank assets have increased while the number of banking institutions has declined. The smallest of the community banks, those with less than $100 million and collectively holding approximately 1% of all industry assets, have accounted for most of the industry consolidation even prior to the 2007- 2009 recession. Banks with more than $10 billion in assets collectively hold approximately 80% of all industry assets. Consequently, profitability and lending activities may differ by bank size.

OVERVIEW OF BANK INDUSTRY CONDITIONS

The banking system has recently seen unusually high numbers of distressed institutions, with failures at rates not seen since the savings and loan crisis that began in 1980 and lasted through the early 1990s.[8] The number of banks that failed, or fell substantially below their minimum capital reserve requirements, increased as the financial crisis of 2008 unfolded. No banks failed in 2005 and 2006, and only three bank failures occurred in 2007.[9] In contrast, the FDIC administered 25 bank failures in 2008, 140 bank failures in 2009, 157 bank failures in 2010, and 92 bank failures in 2011. In 2012, there were 51 bank failures.[10]

2000-2012

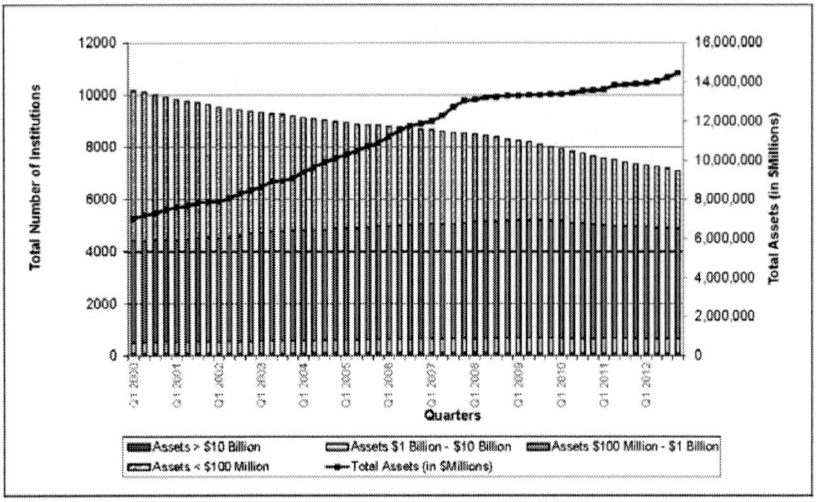

Source: FDIC.

Notes: The number of institutions holding $10 billion or more in assets appears as red dots sitting on the horizontal axis. The number of institutions range from 95 to 108 over the entire period.

Figure 1. FDIC-Insured Institutions by Asset Size and Industry Asset Holdings.

Of the 7,083 FDIC-insured institutions in 2012, the FDIC reports that approximately 35% reported negative quarterly income at various quarters after the financial crisis; the percentage of these unprofitable institutions fell to 10.48% in 2012. The FDIC also maintains a problem list of banks at risk of failure because their capital reserves have fallen below regulatory minimum levels (but perhaps not yet far enough below to be shut down). The number of depository institutions on the FDIC's problem list rose from 52 banks in 2005, peaked at 888 in the first quarter of 2011, before falling to 651 by the end of 2012. The assets of the problem institutions, however, total $232.7 billion, representing approximately 1.6% of total industry assets. Hence, small institutions are likely to still be experiencing financial distress. **Figure 2** shows the number of FDIC-insured banks, the number of problem banks, and the number of unprofitable institutions by quarter since 2005. Note that an unprofitable institution may not also be counted on the FDIC's problem institution list if it has enough capital to absorb its quarterly revenue shortfalls and still meet the *adequately capitalized* or *well-capitalized* thresholds.[11]

2005-2012

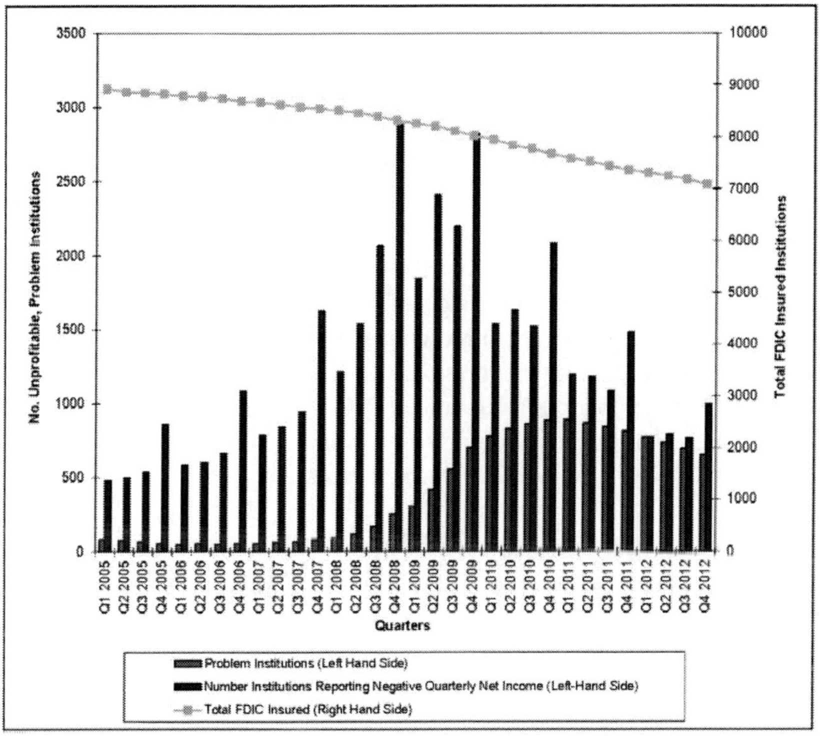

Source: FDIC.

Notes: The number of institutions reporting negative quarterly net income is computed by multiplying the total number of FDIC-insured institutions by the percentage of unprofitable institutions reported by the FDIC.

Figure 2. Total FDIC Insured, Total Problem, Total Unprofitable Institutions.

The industry is returning to profitability. The FDIC reports that industry net income rose to $141.3 billion, representing the highest net income level since 2006.[12] Although lending growth has increased, the FDIC reports that most of the earnings increase can be attributed to increases in noninterest (fee) income and lower provisions set aside for anticipated loan losses, which will be discussed below.

Return on assets (RoA) and return on equity (RoE) are commonly used metrics to gauge bank profitability. RoA is computed with net income (total assets minus total liabilities) in the numerator and average total assets in the denominator. The RoA measures the financial return of a bank's average assets or lending activities. Given that the banking industry relies heavily upon borrowed liabilities to fund assets, the numerator of the ratio would be significantly smaller than the denominator; therefore, a RoA of approximately 1% is considered profitable.[13] RoE is computed with net income in the numerator and the total amount of common shareholder equity in the denominator. The RoE is a measure of financial return for shareholders. Unlike RoA, RoE does not have a barometer of "acceptable" performance because it can increase due to either asset profitability or depleting capital positions, making it difficult to establish a benchmark standard.[14]

The FDIC reported industry declines in both RoA and RoE during the 2007-2009 recession as the numerators of both ratios fell even faster than their denominators. The negative returns coincided with the wave of loan defaults that also occurred during the recession, which led to deterioration of capital, increases in the number of banks on the FDIC's problem list, and increases in bank failures. The RoA and RoE measures, which are illustrated in **Figure 3**, have exhibited a reversal in course since the recession.

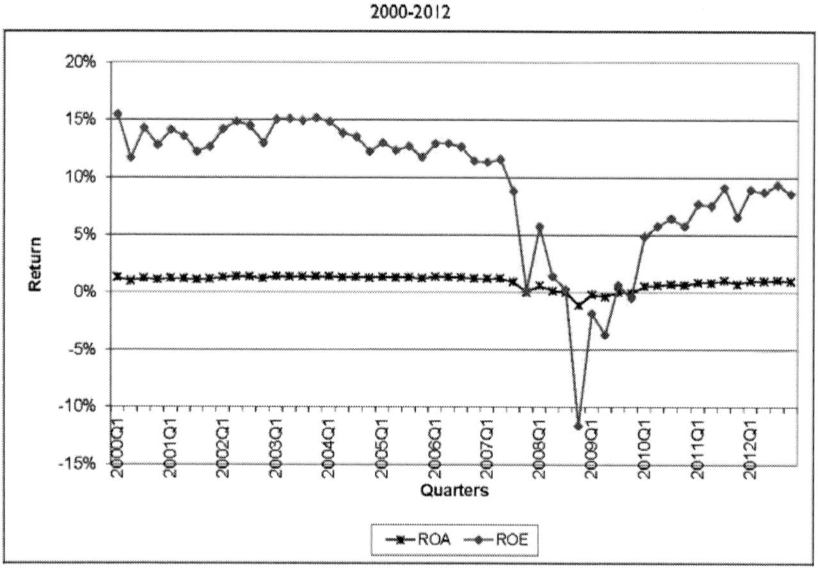

Source: FDIC.

Figure 3. Return on Assets, Return on Equity.

2002-2012

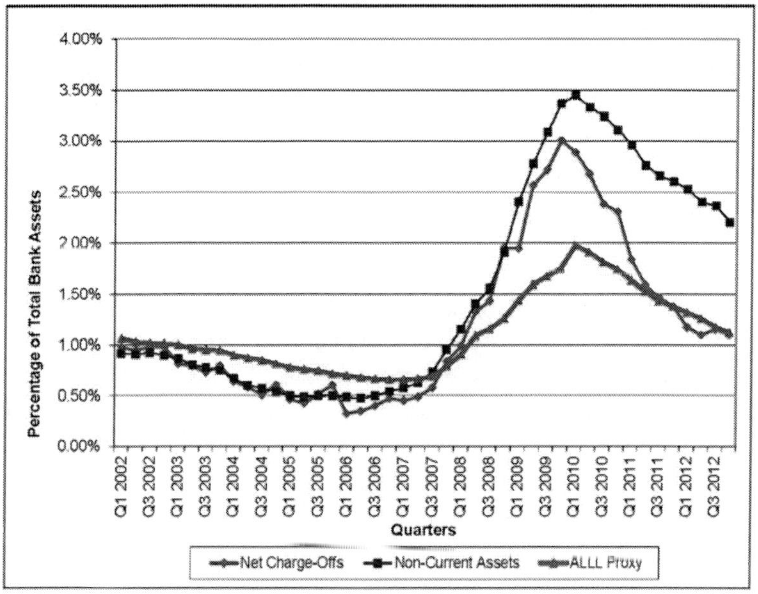

Source: FDIC.

Notes: The ALLL proxy is computed by CRS using FDIC data.

Figure 4. Non-Current Assets, Net Charge-Offs, Allowances for Loan & Lease Losses (ALLL Proxy).

As previously stated, declines in RoA and RoE may be attributed to loan repayment problems that led to an increase in the numbers of distressed institutions. *Non-current assets* are loans that borrowers do not repay as scheduled. The *allowances for loan and lease losses* (ALLL) is a component of regulatory bank capital set aside for anticipated (or estimated) loan losses. *Loan loss provisioning* refers to increasing the amount of ALLL when loan default risks increase; decreases are referred to as *charge-offs* or deductions from ALLL when lenders determine that non-current assets will not be repaid.[15] **Figure 4** shows the increase in both noncurrent assets and charge-offs after 2007.

Banking organizations are required to hold capital for both anticipated and unanticipated default risks. The federal bank regulators believe that most banking organizations already hold sufficient capital to meet the proposed higher requirements to buffer against *unanticipated* losses.[16] On the other hand, ALLL requirements change more frequently (quarterly) or when expected credit losses may have increased. Hence, a bank may have sufficient capital to meet unanticipated defaults, which may be associated with unforeseen events (such as a sudden increase in the unemployment rate), but it may still need to increase ALLL provisions should a borrower begin showing signs of repayment difficulties that may go into default. If banks can absorb anticipated loan losses using current income earnings, their capital will be left intact for unanticipated losses.

The FDIC reports a continued decline in aggregate ALLL provisioning as of 2012.[17] As mentioned earlier, the FDIC reported that lower levels of provisions that were set aside for distressed loans was an important factor in determining industry profitability in 2012. The ratio of aggregate ALLL provisioning to total bank assets, also shown in **Figure 4**, is an ALLL proxy indicating that loan loss provisioning matched and often exceeded the *anticipated* percentage of problem assets prior to 2007, which are composed of net charge-offs and non-current assets.[18] The ALLL indicator suggests that the amount of loan loss provisioning after the end of 2012 appears to cover net charge-offs; however, the percentage of non-current loans must decline even more relative to the current level of ALLL provisioning (or ALLL provisioning must increase more) before the industry can fully cover its anticipated default risks.

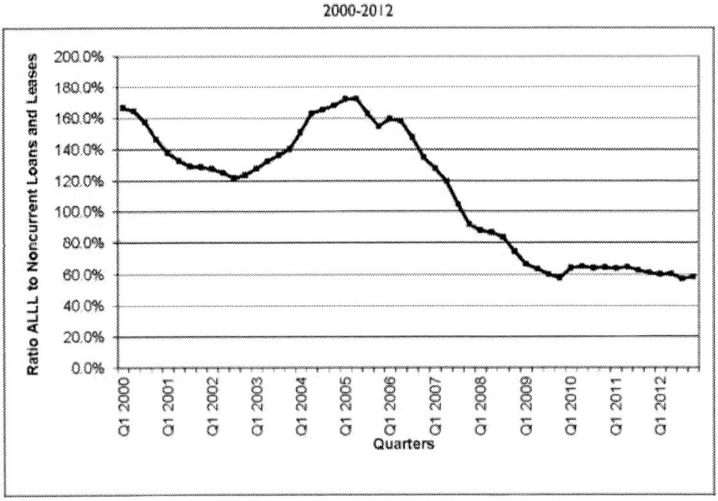

Source: FDIC.

Figure 5. Coverage Ratio.

Although the ALLL indicator in **Figure 4** was constructed for illustrative purposes, the *coverage ratio*, which is defined as the amount of loan loss reserves and equity per dollar of noncurrent loans, is more commonly used to assess the extent of non-performing assets relative to ALLL levels.[19] Despite industry efforts to increase loan loss provisioning, the more rapid pace of non-current loans led to a substantial decline in the industry coverage ratio, shown in **Figure 5**. A coverage ratio below 100% indicates that there is insufficient ALLL to cover weak loans that could go into further distress. Consequently, regulators are requiring banks to increase loan loss provisioning (as well as other components of regulatory capital) to levels that better match the levels of problem loans.[20]

As regulators have taken measures to restore ALLL and other components of bank capital to higher levels, the growth rate of bank lending portfolios is likely to be affected. Similarly, a weak demand for loans or decline in the number of borrowers deemed creditworthy can also cause banks to make fewer loans, meaning that asset portfolios would grow at a slower pace.[21] The asset growth rate is computed as the percentage change in total assets from quarter to quarter, and is shown in **Figure 6**. The asset growth rate fell below negative 2% beginning in the first quarter of 2009, which had not occurred since the 1990-1991 recession[22], and remained negative until a year later; 2010 also saw negative asset growth during the second and fourth quarters. Given the magnitude of loan repayment problems, banks grew more cautious about lending (or growing their asset portfolios) to avoid the risk of further weakening their ALLL and capital reserve positions, which are more difficult to keep in regulatory compliance in a distressed environment. Consequently, although the rate of bank lending has increased since the recession, it has not returned to pre-recessionary levels despite the industry's return to profitability.

OVERVIEW OF REVENUE COMPOSITION BY BANK SIZE

As previously stated, banks typically borrow funds from depositors for shorter periods of time relative to their originated loans. Banks must continuously renew their short-term borrowings until longer-term loans have been fully repaid. For example, suppose a bank originates a consumer loan that is expected to be repaid in full over two years. Over the two years that the loan is being repaid, the bank will simultaneously "fund the loan," meaning that it will treat its depositors' funds as a sequence of quarterly (for a total of eight quarters) or monthly (for a total of 24 months) short-term loans and make periodic interest payments to depositors.[23] The spread or difference between lending long and borrowing short is known as the *net interest margin.*

Smaller banks typically engage in "relationship banking," meaning that they develop close familiarity with their respective customer bases and typically provide financial services within a circumscribed geographical area. Relationship banking allows these institutions to capture lending risks that are unique, infrequent, and localized. These institutions, which rely heavily on commercial (real estate and retail) lending and funding with deposits, typically have higher net interest margins than large banks. Funding loans with deposits is cheaper than accessing the short-term financial markets, particularly for small institutions that do not have the transaction volume or size to justify the higher costs.

In contrast, large institutions typically engage in "transactional banking" or high-volume lending that employs automated underwriting methodologies that often cannot capture atypical lending risks.[24] Large banks are not as dependent upon deposits to fund their lending activities given their greater ability to access short-term money markets. Large banks typically have lower spreads because their large-scale activities generate large amounts of fee income from a wide range of activities, which can be used to cover the costs of borrowing in the short-term money markets.[25] Revenues are earned by originating and selling large amounts of loans to nonbank institutions, such as government-sponsored enterprises (Fannie Mae and Freddie Mac) and non-depository institutions that hold financial assets (e.g., insurance companies, hedge funds). A large share of fees are still generated from traditional banking activities (e.g., safe deposit, payroll processing, trust services, payment services) and from facilitating daily purchase and payment transactions, in which service fees may be collected from checking, money orders, and electronic payment card (debit and credit) transactions.[26] Hence, transactional or high-volume banking activities allow large banks to generate fee income and engage in financial transactions characterized by minimum deal size or institutional size requirements, which simultaneously act as a barrier to participation by community banks.[27]

Given the differences in the composition of bank revenue streams, the net interest margins and fee income streams are illustrated by asset size categories. **Figure 7** presents the net interest margins (or spreads) by bank size. By 2009, the net interest margins had declined for small banks, but they still remained higher over time than the margins for larger banks. The net interest margins for large banks increased over the recession period as they experienced a large influx of deposits during the recession, perhaps due to uncertainty in the money market; this "flight to safety" influx resulted in a substantial drop in their funding costs.[28] In other words, large banks were able to rely relatively less on short-term financial markets and could, instead, take advantage of cheaper funding from deposits. Although net interest margins may appear to be returning to pre-recession trends, the future performance of this spread would still be affected by any of the following factors. The spread may be affected by an increase in liquid asset holdings (e.g., securities backed by the U.S. federal government), perhaps due to weaker demand for more illiquid loans (e.g., mortgages, commercial loans) or lower capital requirements associated with holding more liquid loans. The spread may also be affected by the amount of deposits that remain or flow out of the banking system as the economy strengthens. Hence, it has become more challenging to predict future profitability arising from more traditional lending activities.

1990-2012

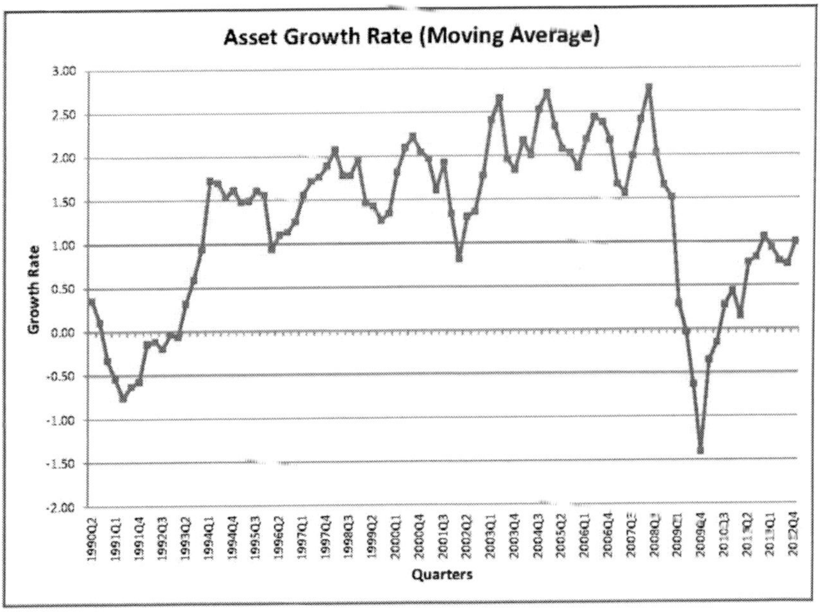

Source: FDIC.

Notes: The asset growth rate is shown as a moving average, which was computed by CRS.

Figure 6. Asset Growth Rate.

2002-2012

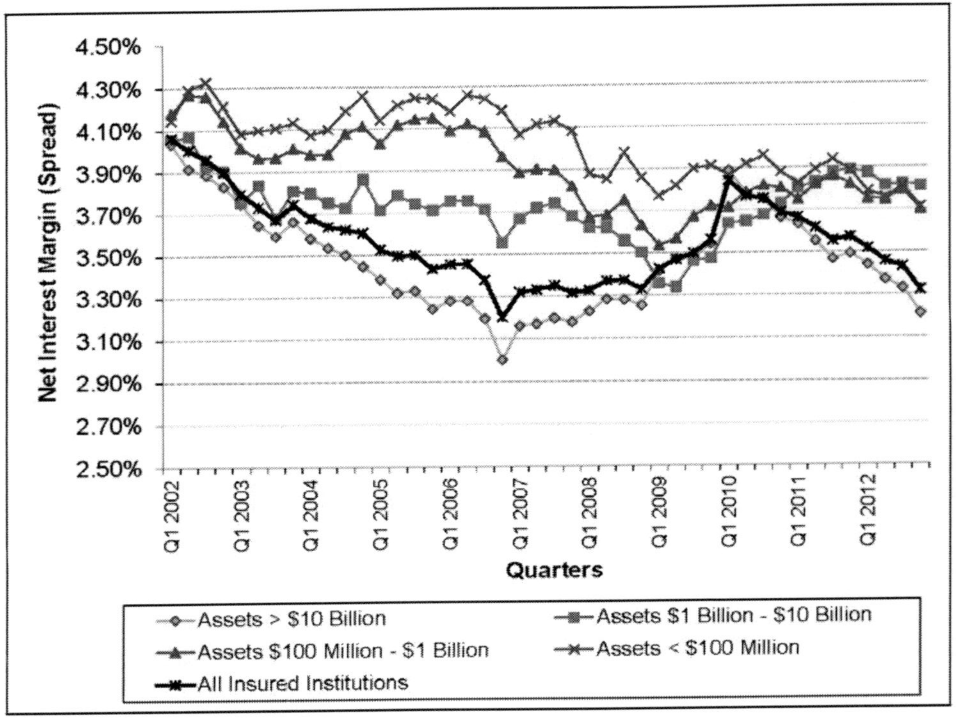

Source: FDIC.

Figure 7. Net Interest Margins by Bank Size Categories.

2002-2012

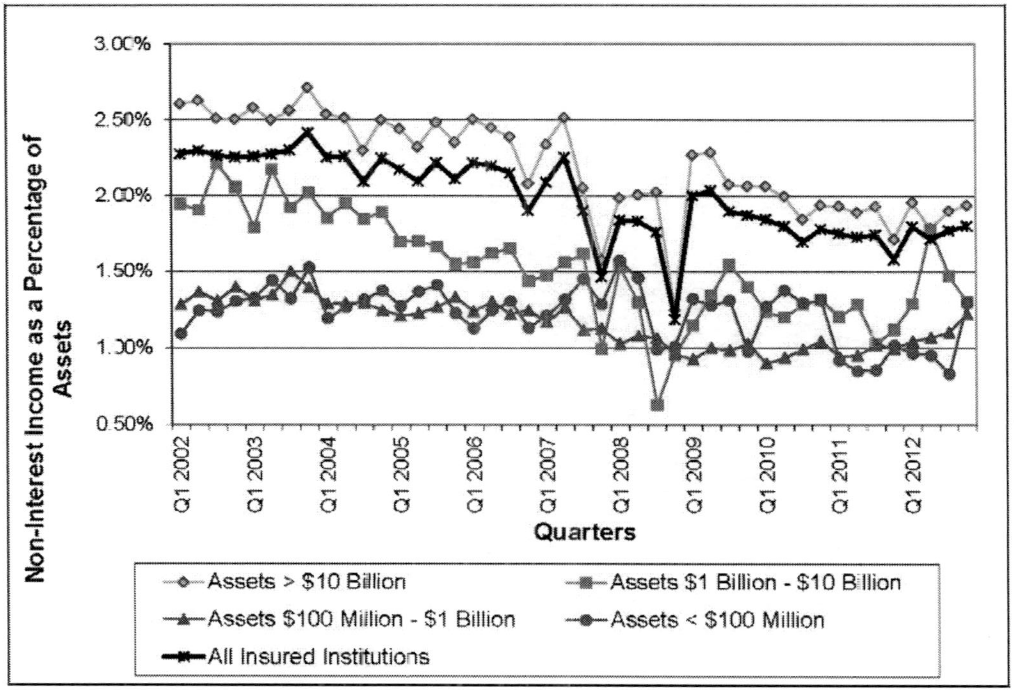

Source: FDIC.

Figure 8. Percentage of Non-Interest Income by Bank Size Categories.

Figure 8 presents non-interest income as a percentage of assets by bank size. As mentioned earlier, the FDIC reported that non-interest was an important determinant of industry profitability in 2012. The overall profitability trend of fee generating activities has rebounded since the recession, but there appears to be more volatility in the fee income revenues of smaller institutions. Although greater reliance upon fee income as a percentage of (large) bank income suggests a reduction in exposure to credit and funding risks, it may not necessarily translate into greater stability of earnings streams.[29] For example, banks no longer collect fees by selling mortgage loans to the private-label mortgage securitization market, which was largely abandoned by investors at the beginning of the financial crisis.[30] In other words, high-volume fee-generating transactions are still dependent upon fluctuations in investor demand for securities that are created from securitized (structured finance) deals, which adds variability to income. In addition, regulatory costs may reduce fee income. Recent regulation of credit card fees as well as on fees that large institutions may collect from debit transactions would affect the earnings streams.[31] Banks would likely seek new opportunities to provide financial services to generate new fee revenues. Hence, future fee generating activities are still affected by financial market uncertainty.

CONCLUSION

The banking industry has exhibited signs of improved profitability since the 2007-2009 financial crisis, but lending has not returned to pre-crisis levels. Bank profitability ratios have returned to positive territory. Net interest margins and fee income as a percentage of assets are less volatile now than when the U.S. economy was in recession. The industry, however, still has more non- current assets relative to ALLL that can absorb potential losses; and there are still many banks on the FDIC's problem list. These factors may be influencing the asset growth rate, which has been positive since 2011, but remains below the average rate of growth observed over the past two decades.

Profitability in the banking industry is not necessarily evidence of a return to previous lending patterns given that the industry is adapting its business model under the new regulatory environment. Lending costs are expected to increase for depository banks as a result of higher overall capital requirements established by the Basel Committee on Banking Supervisors and by the Dodd-Frank Wall Street Reform and Consumer Protection Act of 2010 (P.L. 111-

203, 124 Stat. 1376).[32] Given that large banks are less dependent upon traditional lending activities than smaller banks, the large institutions may be able to generate enough fee income from a wide range of other financial activities to remain profitable even if lending activity does not resemble pre-recessionary levels. Hence, profitability trends may differ for banks by size.

End Notes

[1] Underwriting in banking refers to two types of activities. *Loan underwriting* occurs when a bank performs a (default) risk assessment of a potential borrower to determine whether to extend credit (loanable funds), the amount, and how much to charge the borrower. *Securities underwriting* occurs when a bank agrees to take on the risk of distributing securities (in the form of bonds or stocks) of another entity that wishes to attract outside investors to provide funding. If, however, the bank is unable to find enough interested investors, then it retains any unsold securities and assumes the default risk associated with the entity. The Glass-Steagall Act restricts the securities underwriting activities of depository banks. Depository banks may underwrite federal, state, and local government securities as well as the securities guaranteed by federal or state governments; but they are not allowed to underwrite equity securities (corporate stock). See CRS Report R41181, *Permissible Securities Activities of Commercial Banks Under the Glass- Steagall Act (GSA) and the Gramm-Leach-Bliley Act (GLBA)*, by David H. Carpenter and M. Maureen Murphy.

[2] This phenomenon is known as a bank run. The federal deposit insurance system in the United States was established in the1930s to insure deposits, which helps to sustain public confidence and avoid runs on U.S. banks. See CRS Report R41718, *Federal Deposit Insurance for Banks and Credit Unions*, by Darryl E. Getter.

[3] See Hyman P. Minsky, *The Financial Instability Hypothesis*, The Jerome Levy Economics Institute, Working Paper no. 74, May 1992.

[4] Bank capital levels may become less effective at reducing intermediation risks if lending activities migrate outside of the regulated banking system and are conducted by institutions that do not hold federally insured deposits.

[5] When a bank fails, the Federal Deposit Insurance Corporation (FDIC) typically closes the institution and administers the repayment of depositors. See CRS Report R41718, *Federal Deposit Insurance for Banks and Credit Unions*, by Darryl E. Getter.

[6] Regulators require banks to maintain minimum *capital-asset ratio* levels, thus maintaining the proportional growth of assets and capital. Capital-asset ratios are computed by placing a financial institution's total capital in the numerator of the ratio and then dividing by its total assets, which are usually weighted by degree of default risk. Note that this analysis will focus primarily on the component of capital most closely associated with loan losses rather than discuss the more complex aspects of capital regulation. See Douglas J. Elliot, "A Primer on Bank Capital," The Brookings Institution, January 28, 2010, at http://www. brookings.edu/~/media29%20capital%20elliott/0129_capital_primer_elliott.pdf; and CRS Report R42744, *U.S. Implementation of the Basel Capital Regulatory Framework*, by Darryl E. Getter.

[7] An alternate and more extensive definition of a community bank is associated with its functions as opposed to its asset size. See Federal Deposit Insurance Corporation, *FDIC Community Banking Study*, Washington, DC, December 2012, at http://www.fdic.gov/ regulations

[8] See Federal Deposit Insurance Corporation, Division of Research and Statistics, *Chapter 4: The Savings and Loan Crisis and Its Relationship to Banking*, History of the Eighties—Lessons

for the Future: An Examination of the Banking Crises of the 1980s and Early 1990s, Washington, DC, at http://www.fdic.gov/bank/historical/history/ 167_188.pdf.

[9] See FDIC *Quarterly Banking Report* as of December 31, 2009, at http://www2.fdic.gov/qbp/2009dec/qbp.pdf.

[10] See FDIC *Quarterly Banking Report* as of December 31, 2012, at http://www2.fdic.gov/qbp/2012dec/qbp.pdf.

[11] The italicized terms refer to the capitalization categories established under the Prompt Corrective Action system of bank regulatory rules, which may be found at http://www.fdic.gov/regulations

[12] See FDIC press release at http://fdic.gov/news/news/press/2013/pr13014.html.

[13] See Ricki Helfner, chairman, "On the Release of the Quarterly Banking Profile," Speech at Federal Deposit Insurance Corporation, Washington, DC, September 12, 1995, at http://www.fdic.gov/news/news/speeches/archives/ 1995/sp12sept95.html.

[14] See European Central Bank, *Beyond RoE—How to Measure Bank Performance*, Appendix to the Report on EU Banking Structures, Germany, September 2010, http://www.ecb.europa.eu/pub/pdf/other/beyondroehowtomeasurebankperformance201009en.pdf.

[15] Net charge-offs are charge-offs minus the delinquent loans that recover. Mortgage and credit card charge-offs differ. A credit card loan charge-off can be recognized immediately, but writing off mortgages takes considerably more time. When it becomes clear that a mortgage default cannot be cured, the property is generally seized via foreclosure and must be resold to recover some losses. For more information on the foreclosure process, see Appendix A of CRS Report R41572, *Incentives and Factors Influencing Foreclosure and Other Loss Mitigation Outcomes*, by Darryl E. Getter.

[16] See Department of the Treasury: Office of the Comptroller of the Currency, Federal Reserve System, Federal Deposit Insurance Corporation, "Regulatory Capital Rules: Regulatory Capital, Implementation of Basel III, Minimum Regulatory Capital Ratios, Capital Adequacy, Transition Provisions, and Prompt Corrective Action," 77 *Federal Register* 52796, August 30, 2012 at http://www.gpo.gov/fdsys/pkg/FR-2012-08-30/pdf/2012-16757.pdf; and U.S. Congress, Senate Committee on Banking, Housing, and Urban Affairs, *Basel III*, Testimony of Michael S. Gibson, Director, Division of Banking Supervision and Regulation, Federal Reserve Board, 112th Cong., 2nd sess., November 14, 2012 at http://www.federalreserve.gov/newsevents/testimony/gibson20121114a.htm.

[17] ALLL provisioning declined for thirteen consecutive quarters as of December 31, 2012. For more details on the decline in loan loss provisions, see FDIC *Quarterly Banking Reports* for March 31, 2012 at http://www2.fdic.gov/qbp/ 2012mar/qbp.pdf and December 31, 2012 at http://www2.fdic.gov/qbp/2012dec/qbp.pdf.

[18] The ratio of ALLL-to-total assets in this analysis follows a similar practice found in Luc Laeven and Giovanni Majnoni, "Loan Loss Provisioning and Economic Slowdowns: Too Much, Too Late?" *Journal of Financial Intermediation*, vol. 12, no. 2 (April 2003), pp. 178-197. Loan loss reserve proceeds, however, must come from current income earnings as opposed to total assets.

[19] See James B. Thomson, "Current Banking Conditions, FDIC-Insured Institutions," Federal Reserve Bank of Cleveland, *Economic Trends*, June 1, 2010, at http://www.clevelandfed.org/research/trends/2010/0610/02banfin.cfm.

[20] In addition to responding to higher balance sheet risks, regulators are implementing Basel II.5, Basel III, and the Dodd-Frank Wall Street Reform and Consumer Protection Act of 2010 (Dodd-Frank Act; P.L. 111-203), which collectively will result in higher bank capital requirements. See CRS Report R42744, *U.S. Implementation of the Basel Capital Regulatory Framework*, by Darryl E. Getter.

[21] See CRS Report R41623, *U.S. Household Debt Reduction*, by Darryl E. Getter.

[22] See National Bureau of Economic Research Business Cycle Dating Committee, March 1991, at http://www.nber.org/ March91.html.

[23] For example, if a bank originates a two-year loan at a fixed 6% interest rate and pays depositors a 2% return, then the net interest margin or spread would be 4%. Given that the 6% rate is fixed, fluctuations in short-term interest rates mean that the spread would also fluctuate over the two years that the loan is being repaid.

[24] For more information on automated underwriting, see Wayne Passmore and Roger Sparks, *The Effect of Automated Underwriting on the Profitability of Mortgage Securitization*, Federal Reserve Board, Finance and Discussion Series 1997-19, Washington, DC, 1997, at http://www.federalreserve.gov/pubs/feds/1997/199719/199719abs.html.

[25] See Judy Plock, Mike Anas, and David Van Vickle, "Does Net Interest Margin Matter to Banks?," Federal Deposit Insurance Corporation, *FDIC Outlook*, June 2, 2004, at http://www.fdic.gov/bank/analytical/regional/ro20042q/na/ infocus.html.

[26] See CRS Report R41529, *Supervision of U.S. Payment, Clearing, and Settlement Systems: Designation of Financial Market Utilities (FMUs)*, by Marc Labonte.

[27] See Conference of State Bank Supervisors, Community Banks and Capital: Assessing a Community Bank's Need and Access to Capital in the Face of Market and Regulatory Challenges, December 2011, at http://CSBS- CommunityBanksCapitalWhitePaper120811. pdf.

[28] For more information on the influx of deposits into the banking system, see Paul Davis, "In Cash Glut, Banks Try to Discourage New Deposits," *American Banker*, July 2010, at http://www.americanbanker.com/bulletins/-1023018- 1.html; Office of the Comptroller of the Currency, *Semi-Annual Risk Perspective*, Spring 2012, at http://occ.gov/ publications/ publications by-type/other-publications-reports/semiannual-risk-perspective/semiannual-risk-perspective- spring-2012.pdf. Many depositors may have moved money to larger banks in response to uncertainty in the money markets. For discussions about money market funds falling below $1 per share, see Nada Mora, "Can Banks Provide Liquidity in a Financial Crisis?," *Economic Review, Federal Reserve Bank of Kansas City*, Third Quarter 2010, pp. 31- 68; CRS Report R42083, *Financial Stability Oversight Council: A Framework to Mitigate Systemic Risk*, by Edward V. Murphy; and CRS Report R42787, *An Overview of the Transaction Account Guarantee (TAG) Program and the Potential Impact of Its Expiration or Extension*, by Sean M. Hoskins.

[29] Robert DeYoung and Tara Rice, "How Do Banks Make Money? The Fallacies of Fee Income," Federal Reserve Bank of Chicago, *Economic Perspectives*, 2004, pp. 34-51, at http://www.chicagofed.org/digital_assets/publications/ economic_perspectives/2004/ep_4qtr2004_part3_DeYoung_Rice.pdf.

[30] For information on securitization markets issues, see U.S. Congress, Senate Committee on Banking, Housing, and Urban Affairs, Subcommittee on Securities, Insurance and Investment, *Securitization of Assets: Problems and Solutions*, Testimony of George P. Miller, American Securitization Forum, 111th Cong., 1st sess., October 7, 2009.

[31] See CRS Report RL34393, *The Credit Card Market: Recent Trends and Regulatory Actions*, by Darryl E. Getter; and CRS Report R41913, *Regulation of Debit Interchange Fees*, by Darryl E. Getter.

[32] For more information on the Basel Committee of Banking Supervisors and the Basel III Accord, see http://www.bis.org/.

In: Safety and Soundness of U.S. Banks
Editors: S. B. King and B. L. Carter
ISBN: 978-1-62618-904-1

Chapter 2

U.S. IMPLEMENTATION OF THE BASEL CAPITAL REGULATORY FRAMEWORK*

Darryl E. Getter

SUMMARY

The Basel III international regulatory framework, which was produced in 2010 by the Basel Committee on Banking Supervision at the Bank for International Settlements, is the latest in a series of evolving agreements among central banks and bank supervisory authorities to standardize bank capital requirements, among other measures. Capital serves as a cushion against sudden financial shocks (such as an unusually high occurrence of loan defaults), which can otherwise lead to insolvency. The Basel III regulatory reform package revises the definition of regulatory capital and increases capital holding requirements for banking organizations. The quantitative requirements and phase-in schedules for Basel III were approved by the 27-member jurisdictions and 44 central banks and supervisory authorities on September 12, 2010, and endorsed by the G20 leaders on November 12, 2010. Basel III recommends that banks satisfy these enhanced requirements by 2019. The Basel agreements are not treaties; individual countries can make modifications to suit their specific needs and priorities when implementing national bank capital requirements.

* This is an edited, reformatted and augmented version of the Congressional Research Service Publication, CRS Report for Congress R42744, dated November 14, 2012.

In the United States, Congress mandated enhanced bank capital requirements as part of financial- sector reform in the Dodd-Frank Wall Street Reform and Consumer Protection Act of 2010 (Dodd-Frank Act; P.L. 111-203, 124 Stat.1376). Specifically, the Collins Amendment to Dodd- Frank (1) amends the definition of capital; (2) establishes minimum capital and leverage requirements for banking subsidiaries, bank holding companies, and systemically important non- bank financial companies; and (3) establishes an implementation timeline shorter than that agreed to in the Basel III Accord. In addition, Dodd-Frank removes a requirement that credit ratings be referenced when evaluating the creditworthiness of financial securities. Instead, the Federal Banking Regulators (i.e., the Federal Reserve, the Office of the Comptroller of the Currency, and the Federal Deposit Insurance Corporation) are required to find other appropriate standards by which to determine the financial risks of bank portfolio holdings when enforcing the mandatory capital requirements.

On June 7, 2012, the Federal Banking Regulators announced the final rule for implementation of Basel II.5 and the proposed rule for the implementation of Basel III. As required by Dodd-Frank, the federal regulators implemented risk-weighting methodologies in both sets of rules that would replace credit ratings. Although smaller institutions with total assets under $500 million may still follow some of the regulatory requirements based upon the Basel I capital framework, all banks would be required to use the risk-weighting methodology established by federal regulators in the recent proposed rule. Banks must also increase capital holdings to withstand adverse macroeconomic and financial scenarios. The U.S. federal banking agencies, however, have announced that the proposed rule will not become effective on January 1, 2013.

The call for higher capital requirements on the banking system could arguably translate into more expensive bank credit for borrowers or even decline. Whether higher capital requirements would result in a reduction of overall lending and systemic risk, however, is unclear. Prior to the financial crisis, banks maintained capital levels that exceeded the minimum regulatory requirements and the economy still saw widespread lending. Bank capital reserves may not have been an effective financial risk mitigation tool especially given that a significant amount of lending took place outside of the regulated banking system. Bank capital may grow more effective at mitigating lending risks in the economy given that lending from non-bank sectors has since diminished, but credit availability may also become more contingent upon the transition to the higher capitalization levels.

Overview of Capital Adequacy Regulation

Lending is inherently risky. Banks face *default risk* because their assets consist primarily of loans made to borrowers who may not always repay all of the principal and interest owed. In addition, banks face *funding risk* because they must continuously borrow short-term to *fund* their assets (customer loans).[1] In other words, banks provide longer-term (illiquid) customer loans by borrowing the funds via sequences of shorter-term (liquid) loans at relatively lower rates.[2] Profits are generated from the spread between the long-term rates lenders charge their customers and the successive sequences of shorter-term rates they pay for liquidity until the longer-term loans are repaid in full. Hence, if borrowers default on their loans, then lenders might be unable to repay their shorter-term loan obligations (liabilities) to depositors and other financial institutions.

Lenders also face *systemic risk*. Although economists have not agreed upon a universal definition, systemic risk may be viewed as an increase in correlation among individual default and funding risks, largely due to a sudden loss of confidence (panic) of financial market participants following a liquidity disruption or decline in asset prices.[3] In other words, systemic risk can be thought of as contagion, meaning that liquidity and payment problems affecting one or a few entities may spread and create disruptions in the rest of the market. For example, suppose an isolated default event prompts other financial market participants to re-evaluate their estimates of default risk for similar or related financial activities. If market participants suspect that an observed default event is relevant beyond the directly involved entities, then growing pessimism of creditors of investors can suddenly manifest itself in the form of a market retrenchment.[4] Consequently, financial panics have historically been rooted in the uncertainty about future asset prices (e.g., real estate, stocks, financial securities) while such assets were serving as collateral for an innumerable amount of loans.[5] Furthermore, the severity of a national recession depends upon the amount of lending by the entire banking and financial system prior to the bursting of an asset bubble, particularly if many of the outstanding loans suddenly became "underwater," such that the balances owed were to exceed the current value of the underlying collateral.

U.S. lending institutions that accept federally insured deposits are collectively referred to as depository institutions, and they must comply with *safety and soundness* regulatory requirements.[6] As part of safety and soundness regulation, banks are required to maintain sufficient capital reserves to buffer against default (credit), funding (liquidity), and systemic risks.[7] A bank's capital is defined as the difference between its assets and liabilities. If a bank maintains sufficient capital, a default on one of its assets is less likely to translate into a subsequent failure to repay some of its shorter-term obligations. A capital buffer, therefore, protects bank creditors from loan defaults by bank customers. A bank is considered solvent as long as it maintains capital above a minimum threshold level, and it is considered undercapitalized and faces the prospect of being shut down by its regulator should its capitalization fall below the threshold. Hence, a bank's asset or lending portfolio may grow proportionately with its capital reserves.

The Basel Capital Accords

The work by the Basel Committee on Banking Supervision (BCBS) on the first Basel Capital Accord,[8] Basel I7, provided an international consensus framework for bank safety and soundness regulation. The objective of the first Basel Capital Accord was to promote consistent safety and soundness standards while providing an equitable basis of competition for banking institutions in participating countries.[9] In other words, international regulators were concerned that banks might prefer to domicile in countries with the most relaxed safety and soundness requirements. Unless capital reserve requirements are internationally harmonized, variation in standards may also lead to competitive disadvantages for some banks with competitors in other countries. Basel I established the amount of capital relative to assets, expressed as a capital-to-asset ratio, that financial institutions needed to maintain. Although the BCBS has no authority to compel member governments to adopt any specific standards, U.S. Federal Regulators generally adopt rules consistent with the Basel Accords. The first Basel Capital Accord was published in July 1988 and fully implemented in the United States by the end of 1992.[10]

The safety and soundness regulatory framework for banking institutions that stems from the Basel Capital Accords include

- a *Tier 1* capital component made up of mainly common shareholders' equity (issued and fully paid), disclosed reserves, most retained earnings, and perpetual non-cumulative preferred stock. *Tier 1 capital risk-weighted asset ratios* are generally defined as bank capital (e.g., common shareholder equity) in the numerator and bank assets (typically weighted according to its likelihood of default) in the denominator. Banks must to hold enough capital reserves to maintain the minimum required capital-asset ratios, which would reduce banks' vulnerability to *unexpected* loan defaults.

- a *Tier 2* capital component that includes allowances for loan and lease losses (ALLL), set aside for *anticipated* (or estimated) loan losses. Loan loss provisioning refers to increasing the amount of ALLL when loan default risks increase; decreases are referred to as "charge-offs" that occur when it becomes apparent that loan(s) will not be repaid. ALLL is adjusted quarterly, and these loan loss reserve proceeds must come from current income earnings (as opposed to total assets).[11]
- stress testing, which is conducted to determine whether a bank can withstand losses arising from a severe recession or systemic risk event and still remain adequately capitalized. Stress testing requirements vary by bank size and type of lending activities, and federal regulators require all U.S. banking institutions to analyze the potential impact of adverse economic conditions on their financial conditions or viability.

The second Basel Accord, Basel II, was developed in response to perceived shortcomings, in particular with the asset risk-weighting system, discussed in more detail in **Appendix A**.[12] In the United States, Basel II was initially applied to only the 19 largest banking institutions.[13] On December 7, 2007, the Federal Banking Regulators published the final regulations to implement Basel II, which became effective on April 1, 2008.[14] The date of expected compliance with some Basel II rules, however, was delayed or waived after the financial turmoil began in 2007.[15]

In response to the 2007-2009 global financial crisis, the BCBS issued what is referred to as Basel II.5 as an amendment to Basel II.[16] Basel II.5 is designed to better capture credit risk in the "trading book" of a bank. The trading book refers to securities that a bank would *not* hold to maturity and would also be accounted for at current market value. A security held to maturity is accounted for in the "banking book" at its original book value, unless the bank decides to sell it; if so, it then moves over to the trading book where it is given fair market value accounting treatment. Distinguishing between assets that should be held in the trading and banking books is not always easy, which makes it difficult to determine the proper accounting and risk weighting treatment.[17] Nonetheless, Basel II.5 is intended to prevent strategic but inappropriate placement of securities in the book that would provide the most favorable accounting treatment of securities at a particular point in time. Regulatory arbitrage can result in a bank having an insufficient capital buffer to mitigate lending risks. Federal Banking Regulators issued proposed rules on the adoption of Basel II.5 revisions in the United States on January 11, 2011;[18] these were amended and re-proposed on December 7, 2011.[19] The final rule on the adoption of Basel II.5, also known as the market capital risk rule, was issued by the Federal Banking Regulators on June 7, 2012.[20]

In a further response to the financial crisis, the Basel III regulatory framework reforms Basel II by revising the definition of regulatory capital and increasing the amount that banks are required to hold. Basel III also requires banks to hold a greater percentage of their assets in cash or in assets that can easily be converted to cash. The quantitative requirements and phase-in schedules for Basel III were approved by the 27-member jurisdictions and 44 central banks and supervisory authorities on September 12, 2010. Basel III compliance requires banks to satisfy all of these enhanced requirements by 2019. On June 7, 2012, the regulators issued a proposed rule to implement Basel III in the United States.[21]

Enhanced Safety and Soundness Requirements under Dodd-Frank

The Dodd-Frank Wall Street Reform and Consumer Protection Act of 2010 (Dodd-Frank Act; P.L. 111-203) also addressed capital reserve requirements for banks. The statutory requirements are summarized below.

Removal of References to Credit Ratings

Section 939 of Dodd-Frank requires the removal of any regulatory references to credit ratings.[22] Given the viewpoint that flawed credit ratings may have contributed to the housing bubble, Dodd- Frank reduced "over-reliance" on ratings and encouraged investors to conduct their own analysis.[23] Section 939A required each federal agency to review regulations that would require the use of an assessment of the creditworthiness of a security or money market instrument, and any references to, or requirements in, those regulations regarding credit ratings within one year of enactment (by July 21, 2011). After review, the agencies had to modify all regulations such that any reference to or requirement for reliance on credit ratings was removed. Regulators were required to find other appropriate standards by which to determine the financial risks of bank portfolio holdings while enforcing the mandatory capital requirements, and they must also transmit reports to Congress that contain descriptions of all regulatory modifications made pursuant to the section.[24]

Section 171: The Collins Amendment

The Collins Amendment of Dodd-Frank provides for the development of capital requirements for all insured depository institutions, depository institution holding companies, and systemically important non-bank financial companies.[25] Small bank holding companies with less that $500 million in assets are exempt from the Collins Amendment. In addition, the amendment would not apply to foreign parents of bank and thrift holding companies; Federal Home Loan Banks would also be exempt from these requirements.

Section 171(b) of the Collins Amendment requires Federal Banking Regulators to apply to U.S. bank holding companies and other systemically significant nonbank financial companies the same minimum-leverage capital and risk-based capital requirements that apply to federally insured depository institutions. Specifically, Section 171(b)(2) says,

> The appropriate Federal banking agencies shall establish minimum risk-based capital requirements on a consolidated basis for insured depository institutions, depository institution holding companies, and nonbank financial companies supervised by the Board of Governors. The minimum risk-based capital requirements established under this paragraph shall not be less than the generally applicable risk-based capital requirements, which shall serve as a floor for any capital requirements that the agency may require, nor quantitatively lower than the generally applicable risk-based capital requirements that were in effect for insured depository institutions as of the date of enactment of this Act.

In other words, the capital requirements of a bank holding company can be no less than the requirements of its depository subsidiary. In addition, the minimum requirements cannot be quantitatively lower than the capital requirements that were in effect when Dodd-Frank was enacted (July 2010). Hence, only the features of Basel I and Basel II that were implemented in the United States at that time, along with other requirements consistent with Section 38 of the Federal Depository Insurance Act, became a floor for future regulatory ratios.[26] Regulators may set higher (but never lower) ratio requirements than those established for insured depositories that were in effect at that time. On June 28, 2011, the Federal Banking Regulators announced the final rule establishing the two floors that went into effect on July 28, 2011.[27]

The Collins Amendment also had the effect of excluding a class of securities from the definition of eligible Tier 1 capital. *Trust preferred securities* are hybrid instruments possessing characteristics typically associated with debt obligations; issuers, however, may have an incentive to redeem at some future date.[28] Basel III, however, requires that only perpetual securities, such as common stock that generally has no maturity date or incentive to redeem, will be counted as (Tier 1) capital. Given that trust preferred securities were excluded from Tier 1 capital for insured depositories at the time of passage, the Collins Amendment effectively makes this a requirement for large bank holding companies and systemically important nonbanks; small institutions with assets of less than $500 million that are not engaged in significant non-banking activities or off- balance sheet activities are exempt from this requirement.[29] Covered institutions also have three years from the July 2010 enactment date of Dodd-Frank to comply.[30]

U.S. Implementation of Basel II.5, Basel III, and Harmonization with Dodd-Frank

As previously stated, the final rule for implementation of Basel II.5 and the proposed rule for the implementation of Basel III, which will be referred to as Basel III NPR (Notice of Proposed Rulemaking), were both announced on June 12, 2012. In light of Section 939A of Dodd-Frank, U.S. implementation of Basel II.5 and Basel III do not depend on credit ratings. Federal regulators have implemented a system that assigns risk weights to various types of asset holdings (or exposures) based upon various categories of loans, issuers (of financial securities), and borrower underwriting requirements. All bank assets (loans) would be multiplied by the assigned risk weight, and the sum of the risk-weighted assets would then be multiplied by a minimum capital percentage to determine how much capital a bank must hold. Although banks having under $500 million in assets would be able to follow Basel I guidelines for determining their final regulatory capital levels, smaller institutions would likely also see an increase in their capital requirements. Given that all banks must follow the same risk-weighting guidelines, the sum of banks' risk-weighted assets is likely to increase even if the same (Basel I) minimum capital percentages are applied. The risk-weighting issues are discussed in **Appendix A**.

After risk-weighting bank assets, the amount of required capital that must be held for assets in the trading book and the banking book can be determined. The final market capital rule, which implements Basel II.5, applies to the trading books of banks with aggregated trading assets and trading liabilities equal to 10% or more of quarter-end total assets or $1 billion or more. For all assets held in the banking books of banks with $500 million or more in assets, the Basel III NPR provides the guidance with the risk-weighting methodology and the required capital levels. The Basel III NPR also incorporates the enhanced capital and liquidity requirements mandated by Dodd-Frank.[31] The computations of the regulatory capital ratios are discussed in **Appendix B**. **Appendix C** discusses the increase in stress testing requirements for all U.S. banks, which may result in banks holding levels of required capital that would likely exceed the Basel III NPR minimum compliance thresholds.

The U.S. federal banking agencies have announced that the proposed Basel III NPR will not become effective on January 1, 2013.[32]

Do Higher Capital Requirements Curb Lending, (Systemic) Risks, or Both?

In theory, increasing safety and soundness requirements in the form of holding more capital should increase the capacity of the banking system to absorb losses associated with its various financial risks. Given that funding loans via the short-term interbank loan markets is typically cheaper than funding them with shareholder equity, banks are reluctant to hold larger amounts of capital than is absolutely necessary. A bank typically must pay its shareholders a greater return than it would to short-term creditors because (1) its return on equity must be competitive with that of other publicly-traded firms; and (2) shareholders require greater compensation for their willingness to shoulder greater default risk. Investors could possibly interpret a bank's decision to raise capital as a sign that its default or funding risks may be increasing.[33] If investors subsequently react negatively to a bank's efforts to raise capital (by seeking higher investment returns elsewhere), then the bank's share price might fall and the risk of bank failure, ironically, could increase.

A bank may attempt to meet increased capital requirements by shifting the higher cost burdens on its customers (borrowers) rather than on existing shareholders. For example, a bank may avoid raising new capital and diluting shareholder equity by reducing portfolio assets (loans), meaning that it may decide to sell some existing assets or reduce future lending.[34] A bank could also pass its higher funding costs on to borrowers by increasing either lending rates or its strategic focus on higher interest rate (unsecured) lending. Hence, a bank must decide how to distribute the costs of higher capital requirements between its shareholders and customers. The distribution of those costs may dampen credit expansion and, therefore, slow the pace of economic recovery.

Although higher capital and stress testing (discussed in **Appendix C**) requirements may provide a larger cushion to absorb unexpected losses, the extent to which a systemic risk event can be mitigated is unclear. Prior to the recent financial crisis, many banks held more than enough capital to be considered well capitalized by regulatory standards.[35] Hence, holding precautionary capital did not necessarily restrain lending by the covered institutions. According to the "paradox of financial instability," the financial system appears at its most robust when it is actually most at risk.[36] The evidence for the paradox is linked to the observation that bank capital is *procyclical*, meaning that it rises during healthy economic periods, when there are fewer defaults, and declines during financial downturns when defaults increase.[37]

Given this procyclicality, bank capital levels have been not so much a reliable predictor of a systemic event but have tended, instead, to be a lagging indicator of distress.[38] Ironically, excessive lending activity may arise when banking institutions grow overconfident as a result of (1) being well-capitalized and (2) as optimism grows with the exceptional performance of an asset used as collateral for loans.[39] Bank capital reserve holdings prior to the recent financial crisis may arguably provide evidence that capitalization levels do not predict or prevent the occurrence of a systemic risk event. In light of many banking crises being explained by the bursting of asset bubbles, which have proven difficult for the Federal Reserve to identify and eliminate, a rise in the pace of aggregate lending activity (especially as lenders' credit risk exposures grow more correlated with the performance of a particular financial market) may arguably serve as a better indicator of vulnerability to a systemic risk event than higher capital requirements.[40]

Bank capital levels may also become more misleading or less effective at mitigating financial risks when a significant amount of lending occurs outside the regulated banking system. Prior to the recent financial crisis, many loans were originated by nonbank (nondepository) institutions and nonbank subsidiaries of bank holding companies; some nonbanks and securitizers that held mortgage loans were not subject to safety and soundness capital requirements.[41] When large amounts of lending activity occur outside of the regulated financial system, raising capital requirements on regulated depository institutions would not necessarily reduce overall financial risks in the economy.[42] Conversely, if non-bank lending activities substantially decline, then the influence of higher bank capital requirements on overall lending activity may increase, causing credit availability in the economy to become more contingent on (or sensitive to) changes in bank capitalization levels.[43]

APPENDIX A. ASSET RISK-WEIGHTING

Capital adequacy regulation requires banks to hold enough reserves to maintain minimum levels of capital-asset ratios, which are generally defined as bank capital (e.g., common shareholder equity) in the numerator and bank assets in the denominator. Basel I introduced a risk-weighting system that weights (multiplies) the assets in the denominator of the capital-asset ratio by a factor that attempts to capture the relative credit or default risk of bank assets.[44] In the United States, bank assets are assigned into four categories (buckets) that receive fixed weights of 0%, 20%, 50%, and 100%, respectively.[45] The risk-weighting system arguably correlates lower credit risk with liquidity, as it typically assigns lower weights to more liquid assets and higher weights to less liquid assets. For example, cash and U.S. Treasury securities, which are liquid and considered to have zero default risk, receive a risk weight of 0%. These asset holdings would have no effect on a bank's portfolio capital-asset ratio. On the other hand, a loan secured by residential property receives a risk weight of 50%, and a commercial loan receives a risk weight of 100%. Loans with higher risk weights reduce the overall portfolio capital-asset ratio by increasing the size of the denominator. A bank holding a loan that is assigned 100% risk weight would be required to hold 8% of the value of that asset as capital. Should a bank decide to hold less cash and increase its holdings of higher yielding, less liquid loans, then its capital reserves must also increase for its capital-asset ratio to remain intact. Conversely, when capital-asset ratios are low, academic research has found that some banks will substitute toward low risk-weighted asset categories to restore the ratio.[46] The composition of a bank's asset portfolio, therefore, may be influenced by the fixed risk weights assigned to the various assets.

The Basel I weighting system arguably did not sufficiently differentiate among the degrees of risk. To illustrate, Basel I places the same capital charge on all commercial loans regardless of the differences in credit (default) risk. In other words, a bank would be required to hold the same percentage of capital against two commercial loans regardless if one were of relatively higher credit quality relative. Furthermore, the weighting system is unable to capture offsetting risk exposures. The capital surcharge is the same even though holding the loan with lower default risk may compensate for holding the higher risk loan. Hence, banks arguably have an incentive to make higher risk loans with potentially higher yields as opposed to those with lower yields.

Another concern regarding the Basel I weighting system is that banks would be incentivized to hold government securities (e.g., U.S. Treasuries) rather than extend loans where credit shortages may exist, particularly during economic downturns. The government securities of nations that are members of the Organization for Economic Co-operation and Development (OECD) receive a risk weight of 0%. Suppose capital-asset ratios fall below regulatory threshold levels during recessions after an increase in borrower loan defaults. If banks, as discussed earlier, previously had the incentive to hold lower quality loans during an expansionary economic period, they may decide to hold more OECD country sovereign debt rather than make new loans during recessionary periods to keep capital-asset ratios in compliance. These actions may further curtail lending to segments where more severe credit shortages may exist, such as in non-OECD emerging market economies or in the private sector when entering the recovery phase of a business cycle.[47] Hence, the Basel I weighting system that relies on fixed weights results in "procyclical" capital requirements, which means they may incentivize excessive risk taking during expansions and discourage credit availability during economic downturns.[48] A bank's risk exposure may also be *understated* should the default risk of OECD country sovereign (debt) securities increase.[49]

Basel II revised the weighting system to allow for more risk differentiation, specifically by adding more risk weight categories. Given that fixed weights do not vary when financial risks change, Basel II also proposed the use of external credit assessments or ratings to support the determination of the appropriate risk weight assignment.[50] For example, suppose a Nationally Recognized Statistical Rating Organization (NRSRO) gave its highest investment grade rating to a security that still receives a 100% risk weight under Basel I. The highly rated security could receive a 20% risk weight under Basel II, which arguably better reflects the high credit quality. A residential mortgage that would have received a 50% risk weight under Basel I could receive a higher risk weight if the borrower has a high loan-to-value ratio (or made a low downpayment). Second or junior mortgage liens receive higher risk weights than primary mortgage liens. The use of mortgage insurance or other financial insurance such as credit default swaps to mitigate credit risk on some loans may reduce the risk weights assigned to those loans.

Given that Dodd-Frank removes the use of NRSRO credit ratings, the Basel III NPR proposes use of a risk-weighting system that allows for more risk differentiation than Basel I. For example, under the Basel I risk-weighting system, a mortgage could receive a risk weight of 50%. Hence, a mortgage loan of $200,000 would have a risk-weighted asset value of $100,000.[51] Under the Basel III NPR, however, the assignment of a risk weights depends upon the loan type and the amount of borrower's equity in the property. The risk weights range from 35% to 100% for a more traditional first lien residential mortgage that has been prudently underwritten,[52] and the range is 100% to 200% for higher risk mortgages (e.g., mortgages with negative amortization features, no documentation); the final weight assigned is inversely related to the amount of the borrower's equity. Although the Basel III NPR risk-weighting system has a greater array of risk weights to differentiate among the degrees of risk, it would still provide procyclical lending incentives for the banking system as previously discussed.

After the value of the risk-weighted asset has been computed, the next step is to multiply the value by the *capital charge* to determine the capitalization requirement. Suppose a borrower purchases a $250,000 home and obtains a $200,000 mortgage, which means the borrower has 20% equity in the property. According to the Basel III NPR, the $200,000 would receive a 50% risk weight, and the value of the risk-weighted asset would be $100,000. For the bank to be *adequately capitalized*, it would need to hold total risk-based capital in the amount of $8,000 (8% capital charge *$100,000) on this loan; to be *well-capitalized*, it would need to hold total risk- based capital in the amount of $10,000 (10% capital charge *$100,000). This example uses only one loan; but the entire balance sheet of a bank is typically risk weighted prior to applying the capital charges, which are discussed in more detail in **Appendix B**.

APPENDIX B. CAPITAL CHARGES AND REGULATORY RATIOS

Basel III, Pillar 1[53] modifies the regulatory capital and liquidity requirements established in Basel I and Basel II, generally in the direction of requiring more and higher quality capital.[54] Specifically, the regulatory reform package revises the definition of Tier 1 capital; increases the amount of common tangible equity held as minimum regulatory capital; establishes a capital conservation buffer; introduces a countercyclical capital buffer; introduces a leverage ratio; and introduces two new liquidity ratios—the liquidity coverage ratio and the net stable funding ratio. The regulatory ratios, sometimes referred to as capital charges, are explained in more detail below. The quantitative requirements and phase-in schedules for Basel III were approved by the 27-member jurisdictions and 44 central banks and supervisory authorities on September 12, 2010.

Stricter Definition of Capital, Higher Requirements

Under Basel III, the definition of Tier 1 capital will be defined more narrowly than at this time. To raise the quality, consistency, and transparency of regulatory capital, the committee determined that Tier 1 capital must consist predominantly of common equity and retained earnings. The financial crisis demonstrated that the resources to cushion against credit losses and write-downs came out of retained earnings, which is a part of a bank's tangible equity base. Hence, the Tier 1 capital definition is now closer to the definition of tangible common equity ratio, which must be above 2% for a bank not to be considered critically undercapitalized.[55] In addition to tangible common equity, the central bank governors added mortgage servicing rights, deferred tax assets, and holdings in other financial institutions to be part of Tier 1. These three assets are considered very liquid and can be sold to offset unexpected losses. These assets, however, should not exceed in aggregate more than 15% of a bank's Tier 1 capital. This requirement limits dilution of the amount of common tangible equity in Tier 1 capital.

To comply with Basel III, banks must meet a minimum common equity capital requirement of 4.5% by January 1, 2015, up from the Basel II level of 2%. On September 12, 2010, the Basel Committee on Banking Supervision (BCBS) approved a capital requirement policy that would increase the total minimum capital requirement (sum of Tier 1 and Tier 2) to 8% by January 1, 2015, three quarters of which must be Tier 1 capital. By 2019, the total minimum total capital requirement will increase from 8.0% to 10.5% at the rate of 0.0625% per year beginning in January 1, 2016.

Capital Conservation Buffer

The BCBS established a capital conservation buffer to encourage banks to build capital buffers outside periods of financial stress that can be drawn down should their assets deteriorate, thus improving their resiliency to unanticipated losses. The minimum amount of the conservation buffer in Basel III is 2.5% of the banks' risk-weighted assets. The capital held in this buffer must be Tier 1 capital. Building this buffer to meet the requirement may occur by reducing discretionary distribution of earnings, dividend payments, and salary bonus payments. According to Basel III, regulators should forbid banks from distributing capital when banks have depleted their capital buffers.

On September 12, 2010, the BCBS agreed to set the capital conservation buffer at 2.5% of risk- weighted assets to cushion against future periods of stress. The 2.5% capital conservation buffer must consist mostly of common tangible equity. The conservation buffer would increase in increments of 0.625% annually. On January 1, 2016, the conservation buffer must be 0.625 and then rise to 2.5% by January 1, 2019.

Countercyclical Capital Buffer

Lending can grow disproportionately when economic activity is expanding and contract when economic activity is contracting, thus feeding and exacerbating the business cycle. On September 12, 2010, the BCBS established a countercyclical buffer that would equal between 0 and 2.5% of a bank's total risk-weighted assets and consist of common equity or other fully loss absorbing capital. The buffer would grow during economic expansions and decrease during contractions. National regulatory authorities will be allowed to determine when lending growth poses a risk to the stability of the financial system and when a countercyclical capital buffer requirement would be necessary.[56] Section 616 of Dodd-Frank requires a countercyclical buffer for all U.S. banks, similar to the countercyclical capital buffer contained in Basel III.

Leverage Ratio

The leverage ratio is defined as gross capital divided by the average total consolidated on-balance sheet assets. Unlike the Tier 1 and Tier 2 capital ratios, the leverage ratio does not depend upon risk weights. The logic behind this ratio is to illuminate financial risks that could be assigned lower weights and still translate into substantial losses. For example, a bank may guarantee payment to a creditor in the event a debt obligation fails to be repaid by a third-party borrower (who requests the bank's guarantee). Given that the third-party loan would not be held in the bank's portfolio, bank loan guarantees would be assigned a much lower weight relative to the loans held in portfolio, yet the bank would be exposed to off-balance sheet default risks. Hence, the leverage ratio assigns the same level of credit risk to all assets (e.g., loans held in portfolio, asset-backed securities, credit-risk guarantees). Banks would be required to maintain a leverage ratio of 3%, which would serve as a capital backstop and ensure that capital does not fall below a minimum threshold.[57]

On July 26, 2010, the BCBS announced a plan to phase in a leverage ratio requirement rather than to approve a specific leverage ratio. During the observation period, the committee plans to put in place rigorous reporting processes to monitor the ratio. Based on the results, adjustment will be made in the first half of 2017 and a minimum leverage ratio will be determined on January 1, 2018.

Section 165 of Dodd-Frank has a leverage requirement; however, this requirement differs from the leverage ratio requirement proposed under Basel III. The term leverage ratio under Basel III refers to an unweighted capital-asset ratio; Dodd-Frank uses the term to refer to a debt-to-equity ratio. Dodd-Frank requires that bank holding companies and nonbank financial companies supervised by the Federal Reserve maintain a debt-to-equity ratio of no more than 15-to-1. Section 115(c) of Dodd-Frank required the Financial Stability Oversight Council (FSOC) to study the use of contingent capital instruments for capital regulation. Contingent capital instruments are bonds with scheduled principal and interest payments that would automatically be converted into equity (or written down) after the occurrence of a predetermined event, thus reducing a bank's liabilities relative to its equity during a period of distress. The FSOC recommends further study on the use of contingent capital instruments rather than implementation at this time.[58]

Two New Liquidity Risk Measures: Liquidity Coverage Ratio, Net Stable Funding Ratio

One definition of liquidity is the ability to sell an asset immediately for its original face or book value without incurring losses or significant transaction fees.[59] Bank portfolios generally consist of illiquid assets (longer-term loans) that are funded by shorter-term loans that must be renewed continuously until the longer-term customer loans are fully repaid. Episodes of uncertainty can cause increases in short-term rates relative to long-term rates, which can translate into distress for financial institutions. For example, institutions holding large amounts of illiquid assets may suddenly find themselves competing to borrow the liquid assets of other institutions, even for a short period of time, which drives up short-term rates. A bank may want to liquidate its holdings of asset-backed securities, but if other banks simultaneously make similar financial decisions, the market for such securities may consist of many sellers and few willing buyers. In both cases, even if banks have sufficient capital reserves and are still considered solvent, the scarcity of liquid funds would result in problems repaying short-term funding obligations. Hence, in addition to having sufficient capital to absorb some loan defaults (credit risk), banks need sufficient amounts of liquidity to buffer against unanticipated reversals in cash flow that could result in asset "fire sales," a phenomenon which occurred in 2007 and into 2008.[60] The BCBS, therefore, introduced two new liquidity risk measures to improve resilience to liquidity stress.[61]

On September 12, 2010, the BCBS established the 30-day liquidity coverage ratio requirement to promote short-term resilience to potential liquidity disruptions. The numerator of the liquidity coverage ratio consists of a bank's stock of high-quality liquid assets, generally government securities and cash, and the denominator measures net cash outflows over a 30-day time period. An observation period began on January 1, 2011, and is set to end in December 2014. During the observation period, the committee plans to monitor the ratio and review the effect on financial markets, credit extensions and economic growth. Based on the results, the minimum liquidity coverage ratio is to be determined and made effective on January 1, 2015.

The BCBS also established the net stable funding ratio (NSFR) to encourage banks to rely upon medium- and longer-term funding of its longer-term loans as opposed to relying primarily upon short-term funding. The numerator of the NSFR would be computed using banks' "available stable funding sources" (ASF) in the numerator divided by assets that "require stable funding" (RSF) in the denominator. The ASF in the numerator would be calculated as the sum of a bank's liabilities and capital using ASF weights. Bank capital would receive a 100% ASF weight; consumer deposits liabilities would receive 70% ASF weight; and shorter-term liabilities would receive lower or 0% ASF weights. In other words, available stable funding sources with longer maturities would be assigned higher weights than those with shorter maturities. The RSF in the denominator would be calculated as the sum of the bank's assets using RSF weights. Cash assets do not require funding and would receive a 0% RSF weight. Loans that mature in less than a year require funding and would receive an 85% RSF; loans that take a year or longer to mature would receive a 100% RSF. In other words, assets that require stable funding receive higher weights the longer they must be funded. The NSFR cannot be lower than 100%. Hence, a bank must either increase its capital reserves if it chooses to fund longer-term consumer loans with sequences of shorter-term loans, or it must diversify the maturities of its own shorter-term borrowings to maintain a NSFR of 100%. The NSFR will not be introduced as a minimum requirement in Basel III until 2018.

On November 4, 2011, Federal Reserve Governor Daniel K. Tarullo indicated that the banking regulatory agencies were making recommendations for changes to the liquidity coverage ratio and mentioned other liquidity alternatives.[62] The liquidity coverage ratio has come under scrutiny, particularly because banks may have to substitute away from originating higher yielding, illiquid loans to hold more lower yielding, liquid assets.[63] The profitability of lending may be impaired, given that compliance may require making fewer loans or funding with longer-term borrowings. In addition, if the banking system held enough highly liquid U.S. Treasury securities to satisfy the liquidity coverage ratio requirements, other financial and non-financial entities may experience a shortage of liquid securities. Moreover, the entire banking system would be more susceptible to a systemic risk crisis if it had a large concentration of liquid (Treasury) holdings that suddenly experienced an increase in credit risk. Hence, the liquidity ratios will have longer time horizons prior to implementation while bank regulatory officials, as well as the BCBS, assess the impact of these requirements on financial markets and make further modifications.

Table B-1 summarizes the Basel III minimum capital requirements and phase-in arrangements. Generally speaking, a bank in compliance with these capital charges would be considered *adequately capitalized.* In other words, the bank has satisfied the minimum levels of capitalization. A bank would need to exceed the capitalization standards in **Table B-1** to be considered *well-capitalized*, and federal regulators have also defined the criteria necessary to achieve that designation.[64] A bank that does not satisfy the minimum capitalization requirements would receive a *prompt corrective action* notice from its primary regulator, which may include penalties and other restrictions.

Table B-1. Basel III Pillar I Requirements and Phase-in Arrangements
(all dates as of January 1; in percentages)

Pillar I Requirements	Years								
	2011	**2012**	**2013**	**2014**	**2015**	**2016**	**2017**	**2018**	**2019**
Minimum Common Equity Capital Ratio			3.5	4.0	4.5	4.5	4.5	4.5	4.5
Minimum Tier 1 Capital			4.5	5.5	6.0	6.0	6.0	6.0	6.0
Minimum Total (Tier I + Tier 2) Capital (row 3)			8.0	8.0	8.0	8.0	8.0	8.0	8.0
Minimum Conservation Buffer (row 4)						.0625	1.25	1.875	2.5
Minimum Total Capital + Conservation Buffer (sum of rows 3 & 4)			**8.0**	**8.0**	**8.0**	**8.625**	**9.25**	**9.875**	**10.5**
Optional: Minimum Countercyclical Buffer (row 6)						.0625	1.25	1.875	2.5
Minimum Total Capital + Conservation + Countercyclical Buffers (sum of rows 3, 4, & 6)			**8.0**	**8.0**	**8.0**	**8.6875**	**10.5**	**11.75**	**13.0**
Leverage Ratio	Mon.							Req.	
Liquidity Coverage Ratio	Mon.				Req.				
Net Stable Funding Ratio		Mon.						Req.	

Source: Basel Committee on Banking Supervision, Group of Governors and Heads of supervision announces higher global minimum Standard, September 12, 2010, p. 7.

Notes: Monitor "Mon." = observation period begins, Require "Req." – introduction of minimum standard. (Ref. No: 35/2010)

APPENDIX C. STRESS TESTING AND SYSTEMIC RISK

A bank stress test is a diagnostic tool used to judge the ability of banks and financial institutions to weather adverse macroeconomic and financial conditions.[65] Stress tests are conducted to determine whether banks and financial institutions remain adequately capitalized and solvent under specific adverse economic scenarios. A stress test may include events such as heightened rates of unemployment, an economic slowdown or a recession, or failure of a large complex banking organization.[66] Such events could result in widespread borrower defaults, the inability to obtain short-term funding, and ultimately, depletion of a bank's Tier 1 capital. Thus, stress tests may alert a bank's management and regulators of potential balance sheet weaknesses during an unfavorable economic or financial scenario. Passing a stress test often requires banking institutions to hold more capital than the minimum required.

Dodd-Frank requires bank holding companies and non-bank financial corporations with consolidated assets of more than $10 billion to conduct and report on self-imposed semi-annual stress tests. The Federal Banking Regulators, however, have delayed implementation of supervisory guidance for stress testing financial institutions with assets of $10 billion to $50 billion until September 2013.[67] Sections 165 and 166 of Dodd-Frank require enhanced prudential standards on bank holding companies with total consolidated assets of $50 billion or more; thus bank regulators will also conduct stress tests for these institutions.[68]

Federal regulators currently require all banking institutions to analyze the potential impact of adverse economic conditions on their financial conditions or viability. Stress testing, however, can vary considerably, particularly for banks of different sizes. Examples of specific stress-testing requirements for small banking institutions and the large complex banking organizations follow.

A Stress Testing Example for Small Institutions

Although community banks are less likely to face the same stress testing requirements as banks with $10 billion or more in assets,[69] they are still required to assess their ability to withstand an adverse macroeconomic scenario. For example, federal regulators, concerned about relaxed underwriting standards in commercial real estate (CRE), increased supervisory guidance for banks with significant concentrations in CRE.[70] Community banks, which typically engage in CRE lending, are generally considered vulnerable to loan defaults and possible failure if CRE prices suddenly collapse.[71] Given that CRE losses can be substantial and federal regulators may not be familiar with the default and funding risks unique to a particular geographic area,[72] the guidance required a bank to submit a plan to its regulator regarding its risk management practices if any of the following conditions hold:

- total construction and land development loans was equal to or more than 100% of its total capital reserve;
- total construction, land development, other land and loans secured by multifamily and nonfarm nonresidential property was equal to or greater than 300% of its total capital; or
- the CRE loan portfolio had increased by 50% or more in the span of 36 months.

The risk management plan must outline the bank's plan to reduce or manage its high level of commercial real estate concentrations. The guidance states its intent to encourage institutions to develop risk management practices and levels of capital levels "commensurate with the level and nature of their commercial real estate concentrations" rather than limit CRE lending by banks. Nevertheless, the regulator would likely require banks with risk management plans that are not deemed acceptable to raise additional capital.

Stress Testing of Large Complex Banking Institutions

In February 2009, the Federal Reserve announced the Supervisory Capital Allocation Program (SCAP) for bank holding companies with assets exceeding $100 billion. Under the SCAP, the Federal Reserve conducted a stress test for the 19 largest U.S. bank holding companies, which included an estimation of their revenues, losses, and reserve requirements under two adverse economic scenarios.[73] The SCAP program conducted stress tests for 2009 and 2010. By November 2011, the Federal Reserve introduced the Comprehensive Capital Assessment Review (CCAR) program that annually evaluates the capital planning process of institutions with over $500 billion in assets.[74] The SCAP stress testing will now continue under the CCAR program.[75]

The stress test scenario developed in the fall of 2011 included a sharp contraction in U.S. GDP, an unemployment rate of 13%, a 50% drop in equity prices, a 20% drop in house prices, and a global recession (to capture the potential of economic stress stemming from Europe).[76] The results from the SCAP were released in March 2012. The simulated total losses that would have been incurred by the 19 BHCs totaled $650 billion; $535 billion would have stemmed from a decline in the value of balance sheet assets and $115 billion would have resulted from a loss of revenue. Only 15 of the institutions would have been able to maintain a Tier 1 common equity ratio of 5% after the adverse scenario.

End Notes

[1] Bank assets, which tend to consist primarily of long-term customer loans, may also consist of cash and other financial securities.

[2] Such short-term borrowing may occur in the form of paying interest on customer deposits or repaying loans obtained in the short-term money markets. The short-term money markets consist of repurchase agreements, commercial paper, and the international short-term market known as the London Interbank Offering Rate (LIBOR) market. U.S. banks may also acquire short-term loans by going to the federal funds market or borrowing from the Federal Home Loan Bank System.

[3] A theoretical framework in economics and finance states that confidence in financial markets rises with profitability; a disruption in profitability may result in a sudden and widespread loss of confidence among market participants and, therefore, a financial crisis. For more information, see Lance Taylor and Stephen A. O'Connell, "A Minsky Crisis," *Quarterly Journal of Economics*, vol. 100 (1985), pp. 871-885.

[4] See Sanjiv R. Das, Laurence Freed, and Gary Geng et al., "Correlated Default Risk," *Journal of Fixed Income*, vol. 16, no. 2 (September 2006), pp. 7-32.

[5] See Gertrude Tumpel-Gugerell, Member of the Executive Board of the European Central Bank, "Asset Price Bubbles: How They Build Up and How to Prevent Them?" Speech at alumni event of the Faculty of Economics at University of Vienna, Vienna, May 3, 2011, http://www.ecb.int/press/key/date/2011/html/sp110503.en.html.

[6] See CRS Report R41718, *Federal Deposit Insurance for Banks and Credit Unions*, by Darryl E. Getter and Victor Tineo.

[7] See Douglas J. Elliot, "A Primer on Bank Capital," The Brookings Institution, January 28, 2010, http://www.brookings.edu/~/media0129_capital_primer_elliott.pdf.

[8] The name, Basel Accord, comes from Basel, Switzerland, the home of the Bank for International Settlements (BIS). In 1974, the BIS established the Basel Committee on Banking Supervision (BCBS), made up of representatives from the monetary authorities of 13 countries—Belgium, Canada, France, Germany, Italy, Japan, Luxembourg, the Netherlands, Spain, Sweden, Switzerland, the United Kingdom, and the United States—to determine and mitigate bank risk in light of different national systems of supervision and deposit insurance.

[9] See Roger W. Ferguson, Jr., "Capital Standards for Banks: The Evolving Basel Accord," *Federal Reserve Bulletin*, September 2003, pp. 395-405.

[10] Basel I was implicitly endorsed in the Federal Deposit Insurance Corporation Improvement Act of 1991 (P.L. 102- 242, 105 Stat. 2236; FDICIA). See William R. Keeton, "The New Risk-Based Capital Plan For Commercial Banks," *Economic Review, Federal Reserve Bank of Kansas City*, December 1989, pp. 40-60 at http://www.kc.frb.org/publicat/econrev/EconRevArchive/1989/4q89keet.pdf.

[11] Tier 2 capital also consists of subordinated debt, limited-life preferred stock and loan loss reserves, and goodwill.

[12] See Secretariat of the Basel Committee on Banking Supervision, *The New Basel Capital Accord: An Explanatory Note*, Bank for International Settlements, Basel, Switzerland, January 2001, http://www.bis.org/publ/bcbsca01.pdf.

[13] The U.S. federal banking regulatory agencies placed banking organizations with at least $250 billion of consolidated total assets or at least $10 billion of on-balance-sheet risk associated with foreign asset holdings under Basel II; these institutions were required to use the most advanced approaches of the Basel II framework to determine their credit risks. See U.S. Department of the Treasury, Office of the Comptroller of the Currency; Board of Governors of the Federal Reserve System; Federal Deposit Insurance Corporation; and U.S. Department of the Treasury, Office of Thrift Supervision, "Risk-Based Capital Standard: Advanced Capital Adequacy Framework—Basel II," 71 *Federal Register* 185, September 26, 2006.

[14] U.S. Department of the Treasury, Office of the Comptroller of the Currency; Board of Governors of the Federal Reserve System; Federal Deposit Insurance Corporation; and U.S. Department of the Treasury, Office of Thrift Supervision, "Risk-Based Capital Standard: Advanced Capital Adequacy Framework—Basel II," 72 *Federal Register* 235, December 7, 2007.

[15] See CRS Report R40007, *Financial Market Turmoil and U.S. Macroeconomic Performance*, by Craig K. Elwell. While providing guidance for Basel II adoption, the Federal Regulators explained that banks could request compliance waivers. See the *Interagency Statement—U.S. Implementation of Basel II Advanced Approaches Framework* at http://www.federalreserve.gov/boarddocs/srletters/2008/SR0804a1.pdf.

[16] The two documents are collectively known as Basel II.5 or "the 2009 revisions" are Basel Committee on Banking Supervision, *Revisions to the Basel II Market Risk Framework*, March 2009, http://www.bis.org/publ/bcbs148.pdf and Basel Committee on Bank Supervision, *Guidelines for Computing Capital for Incremental Risk in the Trading Book*, http://www.bis.org/publ/bcbs149.pdf.

[17] See Basel Committee on Banking Supervision, *Trading Book Survey: A Summary of Responses*, April 2005, http://www.bis.org/publ/bcbs112.pdf.

[18] See Office of the Comptroller of the Currency, Treasury; Board of Governors of the Federal Reserve; and Federal Deposit Insurance Corporation, "Risk-Based Capital Guidelines: Market Risk," 76 *Federal Register*, January 11, 2011 at http://www.gpo.gov/fdsys/pkg/FR-2011-01-11/pdf/2010-32189.pdf.

[19] See Office of the Comptroller of the Currency, Treasury; Board of Governors of the Federal Reserve; Federal Deposit Insurance Corporation, "Risk-Based Capital Guidelines: Market Risk; Alternatives to Credit Ratings for Debt and Securitization Positions," December 7, 2011 at http://www.federalreserve.gov/newsevents/press/bcreg/ bcreg20111207a1.pdf.

[20] See announcement at http://www.federalreserve.gov/newsevents/press/bcreg/20120607b.htm.

[21] See announcement at http://www.federalreserve.gov/newsevents/press/bcreg/20120607a.htm. The comment period was extended from September 7, 2012 to October 22, 2012. See http://www.occ.gov/news-issuances/news-releases/ 2012/nr-occ-2012-118.html.

[22] A credit rating is a third party assessment of the future credit risk of a firm that typically has issued financial securities. See http://www.sec.gov/news/press/2011/2011-59.htm.

[23] See U.S. Congress, Senate Committee on Banking, Housing, and Urban Affairs, *Dodd Frank Wall Street Reform: Conference Report Summary*, 111th Cong., 2nd sess., July 1, 2010, http:// banking.senate.gov/public/_files/070110_Dodd_Frank_Wall_Street_Reform_comprehensive_summary_Final.pdf.

[24] For example, the Office of the Comptroller of the Currency (OCC) asked for comments in November 2011 for alternative frameworks that could be applied to the securities purchased by national banks and federal savings associations. See "Alternatives to the Use of External Credit Ratings in the Regulations of the OCC," *Federal Register*, November 29, 2011, p. 73527, available at http://www.gpo.gov/fdsys/pkg/FR-2011-11-29/html/2011-30428.htm.

[25] For more information on the regulation of systemically important firms, see CRS Report R42083, *Financial Stability Oversight Council: A Framework to Mitigate Systemic Risk*, by Edward V. Murphy.

[26] For more information on the Federal Deposit Insurance Act of 1950 (P.L. 81-797, 64 Stat. 873), see http://www.fdic.gov/regulationsSee Julie L. Stackhouse, *Prompt Corrective Action: What Does It Mean for a Bank's Liquidity*, Federal Reserve Bank of St. Louis, Central Banker, fall 2008, http://www.stlouisfed.org/publications/cb/articles/ ?id=792.

[27] See http://www.gpo.gov/fdsys/pkg/FR-2011-06-28/pdf/2011-15669.pdf.

[28] See http://www.fdic.gov/news/news/inactivefinancial/2002/fil0229a.html. For a discussion of trust preferred securities, see http://www.philadelphiafed.org/bank-resources/publications/ src-insights/2009/first-quarter/ q1si4_09.cfm. Examples of trust preferred securities may be directly issued preferred stocks with the tax advantages of debt, and the preferred stock that the U.S. Treasury purchased under the Troubled Asset Relief Program (TARP). For information about the securities purchased by the U.S. Treasury under TARP, see CRS Report R41427, *Troubled Asset Relief Program (TARP): Implementation and Status*, by Baird Webel.

[29] Off-balance sheet activities refer to risk exposures arising from assets that a bank does not own. For example, a bank may assume some or all of the default risk by providing a guarantee for a loan that it has sold to another institution.

[30] Basel III starts the phasing out of non-perpetual securities in 2013, whereas this period for banks in the United States began when Dodd-Frank became public law, July 21, 2010, which accelerates the compliance schedule.

[31] Safety and soundness provisions of Dodd-Frank that apply specifically to systemically important firms, such as a systemic risk tax, are not addressed in this report. For more information on these topics, see CRS Report R41384, *The Dodd-Frank Wall Street Reform and Consumer Protection Act: Systemic Risk and the Federal Reserve*, by Marc Labonte. The third component of the Basel III NPR, titled "Regulatory Capital Rules: Advanced Approaches Risk- Based Capital Rule; Market Risk Capital Rule," specifically applies to institutions with $250 billion or more in consolidated assets or $10 billion or more in foreign exposure (See http://www.occ.gov/news-issuances/bulletins/2012/ bulletin-2012-24.html); these rules are also not addressed in this report.

[32] See http://www.federalreserve.gov/newsevents/press/bcreg/20121109a.htm.

[33] See William C. Dudley, "U.S. Experience with Bank Stress Testing," Speech at the Group of 30 Plenary Meeting, Bern, Switzerland, May 28, 2011, http://www.newyorkfed.org/ newsevents/speeches/2011/dud110627.html.

[34] If a bank decides to curtail lending to remain in or move toward compliance, it may also have to turn away deposits to maintain proper balance sheet ratios. For information on banks having to turn away deposits, see Eric Dash and Nelson D. Schwartz, "In Cautious Times, Banks Flooded With Cash," *New York Times*, October 24, 2011, http://www.nytimes.com/ 2011/10/25/business/banks-flooded-with-cash Paul Davis, "In Cash Glut, Banks Try to Discourage New Deposits," *American Banker*, July 2010, http://www.american banker.com/bulletins/-1023018-1.html.

[35] See http://www.imf.org/external/pubs/ft/wp/2010/wp10286.pdf. Large U.S. banking firms held significantly more equity capital than the minimum required by bank regulators under the Basel I requirements over the 1992 through 2006 period. See Allen N. Berger, Robert DeYoung, and Mark Flannery, *How Do Large Banking Organizations Manage Their Capital Ratio?*, The Federal Reserve Bank of Kansas City Economic Research Department, Research Working Paper 08-01, April 2008, http://www.kc.frb.org/Publicat/RESWKPAP/ PDF/RWP08-01.pdf.

[36] For a discussion of the paradox of financial stability, see Herve Hannon, "Towards a Global Financial Stability Framework," Speech at the 45th SEACEN Governors' Conference, Siem Reap province, Cambodia, February 2010, http://www.bis.org/speeches/sp100303.pdf? noframes=1.

[37] Section 616 of Dodd-Frank requires U.S. banks to maintain a *countercyclical buffer*, which is defined and discussed in **Appendix B**, to address issues related to procyclical capital movements. Countercyclical capital buffers may increase the capacity of banks to absorb

losses associated with an unexpected rise in defaults or encourage them to increase the cost of credit, which may dampen the demand for credit. In 2008, however, Spain experienced a property bubble and subsequent banking crisis despite the requirement of countercyclical capital buffers for Spanish banks. For more information, see Gabriel Jimenez, Steven Ongena, and Jose-Luis Peydro, et al., *Macroprudential Policy, Countercyclical Bank Capital Buffers and Credit Supply: Evidence from the Spanish Dynamic Provisioning Experiments*, Barcelona Graduate School of Economics, Working Paper 628, Barcelona, Spain, April 2012, http://research.barcelonagse.eu/tmp/working_papers/628.pdf; and CRS Report R42377, *The Eurozone Crisis: Overview and Issues for Congress*, coordinated by Rebecca M. Nelson.

[38] For a discussion of the limitations of stress testing as early warning devices, see Claudio Borio, Mathias Drehmann, and Kostas Tsatsaronis, *Stress-Testing Macro Stress-Testing: Does It Live Up to Expectations*, Bank for International Settlements, Working Papers 369, Basel, Switzerland, January 2012, http://www.bis.org/publ/work369.htm.

[39] See Franklin Allen and Douglas Gale, "Bubbles, Crisis, and Policy," *Oxford Review of Economic Policy*, vol. 15, no. 3 (1999) at http://finance.wharton.upenn.edu/~allenf/download/Vita/bubbles.pdf. For a discussion about overconfidence in the performance of mortgage assets stemming from overconfidence in rising house values, see Christopher L. Foote and Paul S. Willen, "The Subprime Mortgage Crisis," in *The New Palgrave Dictionary of Economics Online*, eds. Steven N. Durlauf and Lawrence E. Blume, Online Edition ed. (Palgrave Macmillan, 2011). In the recent banking crisis, institutions that experience large losses held high concentrations or were exposure to mortgage securities prior to the downturn in the housing market. See David Greenlaw, Jan Hatzius, and Anil K. Kashyap, et al., "Leveraged Losses: Lessons from the Mortgage Market Meltdown," Proceedings of the U.S. Monetary Policy Forum, 2008, http://research.chicagobooth.edu/igm/docs/USMPF_FINAL_Print.pdf.

[40] See Governor Ben S. Bernanke, "Asset-Price "Bubbles" and Monetary Policy," Remarks before the New York Chapter of the National Association for Business Economics, New York, NY, October 15, 2002, http://www.federalreserve.gov/boarddocs/speeches/2002/20021015/default.htm; and U.S. Department of the Treasury, Office of the Comptroller of the Currency, "Concentrations of Credit, Comptroller's Handbook," December 2011, http://www.occ.gov/publications/publications-by-type/comptrollers-handbook/Concentration-HB-Final.pdf.

[41] Large complex financial institutions sponsored financial conduits that allowed mortgages to be financed off the balance sheets of supervised banks. Some critics argue that such off-balance-sheet activities would not have been able to occur had banks not been given permission to participate in a wider variety of financial activities. See Thomas M. Hoenig and Charles S. Morris, *Restructuring the Banking System to Improve Safety and Soundness*, Federal Reserve Bank of Kansas City, May 2011, http://www.kansascityfed.org/publicat/speeches/Restructuring-the-Banking-System- 05-24-11.pdf. For more information on the supervision of Large Complex Banking Organizations, see Lisa M. DeFerrari and David E. Palmer, "Supervision of Large Complex Banking Organizations," *Federal Reserve Bulletin*, February 2001, pp. 47-57, at http://www.federalreserve.gov/pubs/bulletin/2001/0201lead.pdf.

[42] See CRS Report RS22722, *Securitization and Federal Regulation of Mortgages for Safety and Soundness*, by Edward V. Murphy.

[43] The Federal Reserve attributes the tightening of credit to the disappearance of private-label mortgage securitizations, which may have been able to fund creditworthy borrowers unable to satisfy underwriting criteria set by Fannie Mae, Freddie Mac, or the Federal Housing Administration. See Chairman Ben S. Bernanke, "Housing Markets in Transition," Speech at the 2012 National Association of Homebuilders International Builders' Show, Orlando, FL, February 10, 2012, http://www.federalreserve.gov/newsevents/speechSection 171 of Dodd- Frank, which requires the same minimum-leverage and risk-based capital

requirements that apply to federally insured depository institutions to apply to bank holding companies and systemically significant nonbank financial companies, may reduce the funding advantages previously enjoyed by the non-banking sector relative to the bank sector, thus increasing the sensitivity of credit availability to changes in capital requirements.

[44] See "Minimum Capital Requirements" at http://www.bis.org/publ/bcbs128b.pdf; "Risk Weighting Assets" at http://www.fdic.gov/regulationsor http://www.ots.treas.gov/_files/422020.pdf.

[45] See Roger W. Ferguson, Jr., "Capital Standards for Banks: The Evolving Basel Accord," *Federal Reserve Bulletin*, September 2003, pp. 395-405.

[46] See Patricia Jackson, coordinator, *Capital Requirements and Bank Behaviour: The Impact of the Basle Accord*, Bank for International Settlements, Basle Committee on Banking Supervision Working Papers, Basle, Switzerland, April 1999, pp. 1-59, http://www.bis.org/publ/bcbs_wp1.pdf.

[47] See Bryan J. Balin, *Basel I, Basel II, and Emerging Markets: A Nontechnical Analysis*, The Johns Hopkins University School of Advanced International Studies, Washington, DC, May 2008, http://www.policyarchive.org/ handle/10207/bitstreams/11484.pdf. For more information about OECD, see http://www.oecd.org/home/0,2987,en_2649_201185_1_1_1_1_1,00.html.

[48] Jose L. Fillat and Judit Montoriol-Garriga, *Addressing the Pro-cyclicality of Capital Requirements with a Dynamic Loan Loss Provision System*, Federal Reserve Bank of Boston, Working Paper No. QAU10-4, September 15, 2010, http://www.bostonfed.org/bankinfo/qau/wp/2010/qau1004.pdf.

[49] See CRS Report R41167, *Greece's Debt Crisis: Overview, Policy Responses, and Implications*, coordinated by Rebecca M. Nelson and CRS Report R41955, *Standard & Poor's Downgrade of U.S. Government Long-Term Debt*, by Mark Jickling.

[50] See *Part 2: The First Pillar—Minimum Capital Requirements*, Bank for International Settlements, http://www.bis.org/publ/bcbs128b.pdf.

[51] For an example of Basel I risk weighting and total capital charges of an entire sample bank balance sheet, see Appendix of CRS Report R42574, *Credit Union Commercial Business Lending: Key Issues for Legislation in the 112th Congress*, by Darryl E. Getter.

[52] For a discussion of criteria that would satisfy prudent underwriting in the mortgage market, see CRS Report R42056, *Ability to Repay, Risk-Retention Standards, and Mortgage Credit Access*, by Darryl E. Getter.

[53] Basel II introduced the concept of three regulatory pillars. Pillar 1 contains the methodology for calculating the minimum capital requirements for banks, among other requirements. Pillars 2 and 3 of Basel II were added to monitor the rise of unintended outcomes. The second pillar requires banks to maintain management mechanisms to conduct ongoing internal self-evaluation of their risk exposures and compliance with the minimum regulatory capital requirement. The third pillar facilitates market discipline and reporting. Specifically, pillar 3 addresses problems with operational risks, which include internal operation failures, such as poor accounting, legal and compliance failures, poor and fraudulent managers and traders, and security failures.

[54] See Basel Committee on Banking Supervision, *Strengthening the Resilience of the Banking Sector*, December 2009, http://www.bis.org/publ/bcbs164.pdf. This document was an expanded and updated version of an earlier document entitled Basel Committee on Banking Supervision, *Enhancements to the Basel II Framework*, July 2009, http://www.bis.org/publ/bcbs157.pdf.

[55] See the definition of "Risk-Based Capital Groups" in the glossary of any FDIC Quarterly Banking Report, http://www2.fdic.gov/qbp/qbpSelect.asp?menuItem=QBP. The tangible common equity ratio is defined as the ratio of a bank's common equity divided by its tangible assets.

[56] The committee also supports the International Accounting Standard Board plans to issue a set of high level guiding principles that would promote an expected loss approach, which is also less procyclical than the current incurred loss approach. See http://www.bis.org/publ/bcbs164.pdf, p. 8.

[57] For more discussion of the leverage ratio, see http://www.bis.org/publ/bcbs165/splr.pdf.

[58] See Financial Stability Oversight Council, Report to Congress on Study of a Contingent Capital Requirement for Certain Nonbank Financial Companies and Bank Holding Companies, July 2012, http://www.treasury.gov/initiatives/fsoc/Documents/Co%20co%20study[2].pdf.

[59] Economists have various definitions of liquidity rather than a single consensus definition.

[60] See Greenlaw, Hatzius, and Kashyap et al., "Leveraged Losses: Lessons from the Mortgage Market Meltdown," Proceedings of the U.S. Monetary Policy Forum, 2008, http://research.chicagobooth.edu/igm/docs/ USMPF_FINAL_Print.pdf.

[61] This regulatory action may also be considered *macroprudential* in nature given that it would act to alleviate funding pressures that could affect the entire financial system and result in a systemic risk event. See CRS Report R40417, *Macroprudential Oversight: Monitoring Systemic Risk in the Financial System*, by Darryl E. Getter.

[62] See Governor Daniel K. Tarullo, *The International Agenda for Financial Regulation*, Board of Governors of the Federal Reserve System, Speech Delivered at the American Bar Association Banking Law Committee Fall Meeting, Washington, DC, November 4, 2011, http://www.federalreserve.gov/newsevents/speech

[63] See http://www.bis.org/publ/bcbs165/spl.pdf.

[64] See http://www.federalreserve.gov/newsevents/press/bcreg/bcreg20120607a1.pdf, Table 6—Proposed PCA (Prompt Corrective Action) Levels for Insured Depository Institutions not Subject to the Advanced Approaches Rule for determining whether a bank is adequately capitalized or undercapitalized.

[65] Stress testing is also a practice utilized in medicine, nuclear diagnostics, pharmacology, and computer and network systems among others.

[66] For the definition of a large complex banking organization, see Lisa M. DeFerrari and David E. Palmer, "Supervision of Large Complex Banking Organizations," *Federal Reserve Bulletin*, February 2001, pp. 47-57, http://www.federalreserve.gov/pubs/bulletin/2001/0201lead.pdf.

[67] See http://www.federalreserve.gov/newsevents/press/bcreg/20120827b.htm.

[68] See http://www.gpo.gov/fdsys/pkg/FR-2011-12-01/pdf/2011-30665.pdf. Sections 165 and 166 of Dodd-Frank also require enhanced prudential standards to be imposed on non-bank financial companies designated by the Financial Stability Oversight Council. See CRS Report R42083, *Financial Stability Oversight Council: A Framework to Mitigate Systemic Risk*, by Edward V. Murphy.

[69] See http://www.federalreserve.gov/newsevents/press/bcreg/bcreg20120514b1.pdf.

[70] See the announcement of the Interagency Guidance on Concentrations in Commercial Real Estate Lending, Sound Risk Management Practices at http://www.federalreserve.gov/newsevents/press/bcreg/20061206a.htm and the regulatory guidance at http://edocket.access

[71] Community banks are generally small banks that generally have assets of $1 billion, meet the lending needs of a circumscribed geographic area. See http://www.fdic.gov/news/conferences/communitybanking/ community_banking_by_the_numbers_clean.pdf.

[72] See Jose A. Lopez, *Concentrations in Commercial Real Estate Lending*, Federal Reserve Bank of San Francisco, Economic Letter 2007-01, San Francisco, CA, January 5, 2007, http://www.frbsf.org/publications/economics/letter/ 2007/el2007-01.html.

[73] See http://www.federalreserve.gov/bankinforeg/bcreg20090424a1.pdf.

[74] See http://www.federalreserve.gov/newsevents/press/bcreg/20111122a.htm and http://www.federalreserve.gov/bankinforeg/ccar.htm. The bank holding companies that would be

subject to annual stress testing by the Federal Reserve are listed at http://www.ffiec.gov/nicpubweb/nicweb/Top50Form.aspx.

[75] Federal regulators may rely upon the SCAP and CCAR stress testing exercises as models when they imple44ment the Dodd-Frank Act requirements throughout the banking system, particularly for the institutions with $10 billion to $50 billion in assets. See William C. Dudley, "U.S. Experience with Bank Stress Testing," Speech at the Group of 30 Plenary Meeting, Bern, Switzerland, May 28, 2011, http://www.newyorkfed.org/newsevents/speeches/2011/ dud110627.html.

[76] See http://www.federalreserve.gov/newsevents/press/bcreg/20120313a.htm, http://www.ny.frb.org/education 2012/Hirtle_comprehensive_capital_analysis_review.pdf, and http://www. federalreserve.gov/newsevents/speech/ tarullo20120410a.htm.

In: Safety and Soundness of U.S. Banks ISBN: 978-1-62618-904-1
Editors: S. B. King and B. L. Carter

Chapter 3

FEDERAL DEPOSIT INSURANCE FOR BANKS AND CREDIT UNIONS*

Darryl E. Getter

SUMMARY

The federal deposit insurance system in the United States protects depositors from losses that would occur in the event that a financial institution becomes insolvent, meaning that the institution's lending activities did not generate enough revenue to repay depositors their principal and interest. By guaranteeing depositor accounts up to a set limit, deposit insurance may also help prevent "runs," which occur when bank customers lose confidence in the ability of a financial institution to repay its depositors and rush to withdraw deposits. A bank run, or panic, can spread and threaten the solvency of other financial institutions should the public also doubt their soundness, thus suddenly and simultaneously withdrawing deposits from those institutions as well. In other words, deposit insurance aims to promote and help maintain public confidence in the U.S. financial system, particularly at times when some depository entities suffer large losses or become insolvent.

The Federal Deposit Insurance Corporation (FDIC) was established to insure bank deposits as an independent government corporation under the authority of the Banking Act of 1933, also known as the Glass-Steagall Act

---

* This is an edited, reformatted and augmented version of the Congressional Research Service Publication, CRS Report for Congress R41718, dated March 12, 2013.

(48 Stat. 162, 12 U.S.C.). The FDIC is not funded by appropriations; it is funded through insurance assessments collected from its member depository institutions and held in what is now known as the Deposit Insurance Fund (DIF). The proceeds in the DIF are used to pay depositors if member institutions fail.

The Federal Credit Union Act of 1934 (48 Stat. 1216) formed a national system to charter and supervise federal credit unions. The National Credit Union Administration (NCUA), which administers deposit insurance for credit unions, became an independent federal agency in 1970 (P.L. 91-468, 84 Stat. 994). The NCUA is not funded by appropriations, but through insurance assessments collected from its member credit union institutions and held in what is now known as the National Credit Union Share Insurance Fund (NCUSIF). Proceeds from the NCUSIF are used to pay share depositors if member institutions fail.

Beginning in 2008, the number of bank failures increased substantially, and the DIF fell below its statutory minimum requirement. Credit union failures also increased, and five large corporate credit unions were placed under conservatorship by the NCUA. The 111th Congress subsequently provided both the FDIC and the NCUA with greater ability to replenish the insurance funds and stabilize liquidity among depository institutions through a variety of measures. Should insurance claims (resulting from failures) exceed the sizes of the insurance fund reserves, additional legislative action may be necessary for one or both agencies to continue to resolve failed institutions.

Current congressional interest in deposit insurance relates to oversight of how the FDIC and the NCUA protect deposits and address solvency issues associated with their insurance funds. This report provides an overview of the FDIC and NCUA, the status of both the DIF and NCUSIF, and describes the procedures followed to resolve failed depository institutions. Appendixes to this report describe measures taken to reduce the loss exposure and total risks to the funds.

INTRODUCTION

The federal deposit insurance system in the United States, which was established in the 1930s, protects depositors from losses that may result from at least two causes. First, a financial institution may use deposits to fund lending activities that may later prove to be unprofitable, leading to substantial losses that make it difficult to repay depositors. Second, a financial institution may find itself unable to repay depositors if its customers suddenly and simultaneously withdraw their deposits based upon speculation or knowledge about the health of similar or neighboring institutions. This phenomenon is generally known as a bank run. Hence, deposit insurance has arguably promoted and helped to sustain public confidence in the U.S. financial system, particularly at times when depositories have suffered large losses.

As the financial crisis of 2008 developed, the number of failures of depository institutions increased. The Federal Deposit Insurance Corporation (FDIC) administered 25 bank failures in 2008, 140 bank failures in 2009, 157 bank failures in 2010, and 92 bank failures in 2011. In contrast, no banks failed in 2005 and 2006, and only three bank failures occurred in 2007.[1] Funds used to reimburse depositors when banks fail are maintained in the Deposit Insurance Fund (DIF), which is managed by the FDIC. The pace of bank failures has, so far, declined since 2011.

According to the National Credit Union Administration (NCUA), 15, 16, and 12 credit unions failed in 2005, 2006, and 2007, respectively; in comparison, 18 credit unions failed in 2008, 28 in 2009, 28 in 2010, and 16 in 2011.[2] In addition, five corporate credit unions, which provide financial services for retail credit unions, saw severe liquidity pressures and were eventually placed under conservatorship by the NCUA. Funds to reimburse credit union members are maintained in the National Credit Union Share Insurance Fund (NCUSIF), which is managed by the NCUA. The pace of credit union failures has declined since 2011.

Regulators and legislators reacted to (1) the depletion of the DIF that resulted from the surge in bank failures and (2) a temporary dip in the NCUSIF below its statutory level during 2010. For example, regulators increased deposit insurance assessments on member institutions. In addition, the NCUA borrowed funds (which must be repaid) from the U.S. Treasury via the Temporary Corporate Credit Union Stabilization Fund (TCCUSF) to administer the conservatorships of the corporate credit unions. The 111th Congress also provided the FDIC and the NCUA with greater ability to meet the liquidity needs of depository institutions, which are discussed later in this report. Whether additional legislative action becomes necessary depends in part upon the future number and pace of failures of depository institutions.

This report provides an overview of the FDIC and the NCUA, the status of the DIF and NCUSIF, and the resolution procedures that are implemented when depository institutions fail. **Appendix A** summarizes efforts to support the DIF during the recent period of financial distress prior to the passage of the Dodd-Frank Wall Street Reform and Consumer Protection Act (Dodd-Frank

Act; P.L. 111-203, 124 Stat. 1376). **Appendix B** summarizes recent actions taken to minimize losses to the NCUSIF and the credit union system.

DEPOSIT INSURANCE FOR BANKS

The FDIC was established as an independent government corporation under the authority of the Banking Act of 1933, also known as the Glass-Steagall Act, to insure bank deposits.[3] The FDIC insures demand deposit (non-interest bearing) accounts, interest bearing checking accounts, savings accounts, and certificates of deposit.[4] The FDIC also insures funds held in traditional and Roth Individual Retirement Accounts (IRAs).[5] It provides separate coverage for deposits held in different account ownership categories, such as single accounts, joint accounts, and IRAs. For example, the funds in a deposit account and those in an IRA would be insured separately by the FDIC, even if the accounts belonged to the same individual.[6]

When a bank becomes insolvent or fails, the FDIC assumes responsibility for repayment of the principal balance in depositor accounts up to the deposit insurance limits. Typically, most depositors have access to their insured funds within one business day after the FDIC closes the bank. With certain deposits, such as 401(k) accounts and retirement accounts, additional time is required to make an insurance determination, but the FDIC estimates that this should not be longer than several days. In some situations, depositors may also receive a portion of their uninsured funds, depending on the sale of the failed bank's assets, a process which may take one or two years.[7]

Congress has periodically increased the maximum amount of deposit insurance coverage as deemed necessary to enhance public confidence and reduce the risk of bank runs.[8] For example, the Federal Deposit Insurance Reform Act, which was enacted on February 8, 2006, raised the limit on deposit insurance for IRAs from $100,000 to $250,000.[9] The Emergency Economic Stabilization Act of 2008 (EESA; P.L. 110-343, 122 Stat. 3765) temporarily raised the limit on deposit insurance until December 31, 2009.[10] Under the new 2008 deposit insurance limits, an individual checking account may be covered up to $250,000 and an IRA may be covered up to $250,000. An individual having both of these accounts would receive total coverage of up to $500,000 in a single bank. On May 20, 2009, the Helping Families Save Their Homes Act of 2009 (HFSTHA; P.L. 111-22, 123 Stat. 1632) made the increase in the deposit insurance limit effective until December 31, 2013.[11] On July 21, 2010, the Dodd-Frank Act made the increase permanent.[12]

To cover losses or costs associated with bank failures, the FDIC collects insurance premiums from member depository institutions and places the monies in the DIF.[13] The designated reserve ratio (DRR), which is the ratio of total funds in the DIF relative to the estimated amount of insured deposits, provides some indication about the adequacy of reserves available to protect depositors and maintain public confidence. The DRR is required by the Dodd-Frank Act to be a minimum of 1.35% of total insured deposits.[14] Should the DRR fall below its statutorily mandated range, the FDIC is then required to devise a restoration plan to recapitalize the fund. A well-capitalized DIF arguably would help maintain public confidence in the FDIC's ability to protect deposits.

By the end of 2012, there were $7,405.9 billion FDIC-insured deposits and 51 bank failures for the year.[15] **Figure 1** illustrates the evolution of the total amount of FDIC-insured deposits and the DRR. The DRR, which was 1.25% at the end of December 2005, was 0.45% as of December 31, 2012. The DRR movements reflect losses to the DIF as well as a substantial increase in insured deposits. **Figure 2** illustrates the DRR along with the number of bank failures.[16] The FDIC has adopted a restoration plan to recapitalize the DFF to meet the 1.35% minimum requirement by September 30, 2020.[17] **Appendix A** summarizes efforts to support the DIF during the recent period of financial distress.

SHARE INSURANCE FOR CREDIT UNIONS

Credit unions are non-profit depository financial institutions that are owned and operated entirely by their members.[18] *Natural person* credit unions, also known as retail credit unions, hold member deposits, which are referred to as "shares"; interest earned by members is referred to as "dividends"; and the shares may be used to provide loans to members, to other credit unions, and to credit union organizations. *Corporate credit unions* operate as wholesale credit unions, providing financing, investment, and clearing services to retail credit unions. Corporate credit unions accept deposits from retail credit unions and invest them in longer-term assets. Retail credit unions are cooperative owners of corporate credit unions. The *U.S. Central Federal Credit Union*, which is one of the 28 corporate credit unions, functions as a wholesale corporate and provides services to the other 27.

2005-2012

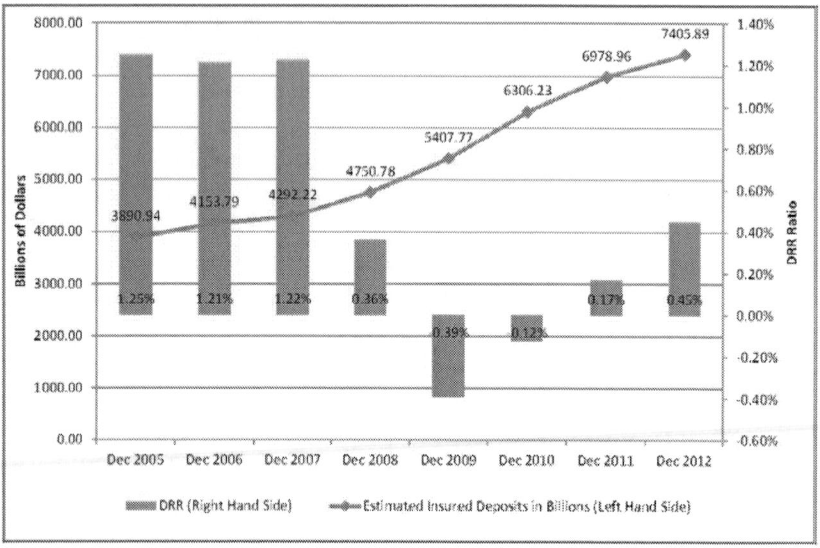

Source: FDIC Quarterly Banking Report.

Figure 1. Total FDIC-Insured Deposits and Designated Reserve Ratio (DRR).

The Federal Credit Union Act of 1934 formed a national system to charter, supervise, and examine federal credit unions; the National Credit Union Administration (NCUA) became an independent federal agency in 1970.[19] Typically, the Office of the Comptroller of the Currency (OCC) charters and supervises commercial banks; the FDIC provides deposit insurance and liquidates failed banks; and the Federal Reserve provides lender-of-last-resort liquidity to solvent banks via its discount window.[20] The NCUA, by comparison, serves all three functions for federally regulated credit unions.[21] All 28 corporate credit unions are federally insured.

Share deposit insurance may help bolster public confidence and prevent panic behavior that can lead institutions to fail, which would require the NCUA to arrange an assisted merger, a purchase and assumption action, or an involuntary liquidation. The NCUA provides insurance coverage for each individual account holder, per federally insured institution, up to the legal limit; funds in IRA and KEOGH accounts are treated as separate accounts that are insured up to the legal limit, per institution.[22] ESSA temporarily raised the basic limit of $100,000 on federal deposit insurance coverage for individual (non-retirement) accounts to $250,000 until December 31, 2009; the limit was made permanent by the Dodd-Frank Act. Retirement accounts retained their existing $250,000 insurance coverage limit.[23]

The NCUA manages the NCUSIF, which was created in 1970 to be the insurance fund for all federally regulated credit unions. Premiums from insured credit unions are the fund's primary source of income. These arrangements are similar to those of the FDIC's DIF. Premiums are used to pay the fund's operating expenses, cover losses, and build reserves. Premiums were originally set at one-twelfth of 1% of the total amount of member share accounts, but P.L. 98-369 required each federally insured credit union to place a deposit with the fund in an amount equaling 1% of its insured share accounts.[24] Examination fees and any penalties collected by the board from insured institutions are also deposited into the NCUSIF. Portions of the fund not applied to current operations can be invested in government securities, and the earnings also generate income for the fund. Hence, the NCUSIF's reserves consist of the 1% deposit, plus the fund's accumulated insurance premiums, fees, and interest earnings.

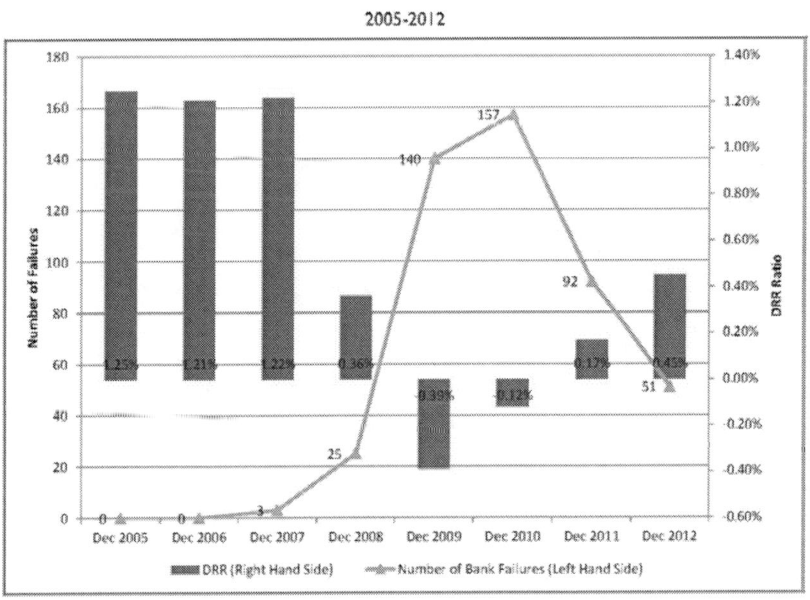

Source: FDIC Quarterly Banking Report.

Notes: Figures are annual or cumulative for the given year.

Figure 2. FDIC Designated Reserve Ratio and Annual Bank Fails.

The statutory equity ratio, which is analogous to the DRR of the DIF, was set by P.L. 91-468 at a minimum 1.2%. The NCUA Board annually determines the "normal operating level" for the ratio of fund equity to insured shares that statutorily must fall between 1.2% and 1.5%.[25] In recent years, the NCUA has set a goal of achieving an equity ratio of 1.3%. The NCUA board may assess a premium when the ratio falls between 1.2% and the declared operating level, and it is required to assess a premium if the equity ratio falls below 1.2%. Similarly, the NCUA board may declare a dividend if, at the end of the calendar year, the equity level exceeds the normal operating level; it is required to do so if the equity ratio exceeds 1.5%. Consequently, a procyclical bias exists with the pricing of NCUA share deposit insurance given the equity ratio cap.[26] Thus, the burden to the NCUSIF, particularly during an economic downturn, depends upon the procyclical bias in share deposit insurance pricing as well as the pace of failures and losses in the credit union system. HFSTHA extends the period of time available to complete restoration of the equity ratio (should it fall below 1.2%) to eight years, which may possibly reduce the amount that assessments would need to rise to restore a fall in the equity ratio below the minimum statutory level.

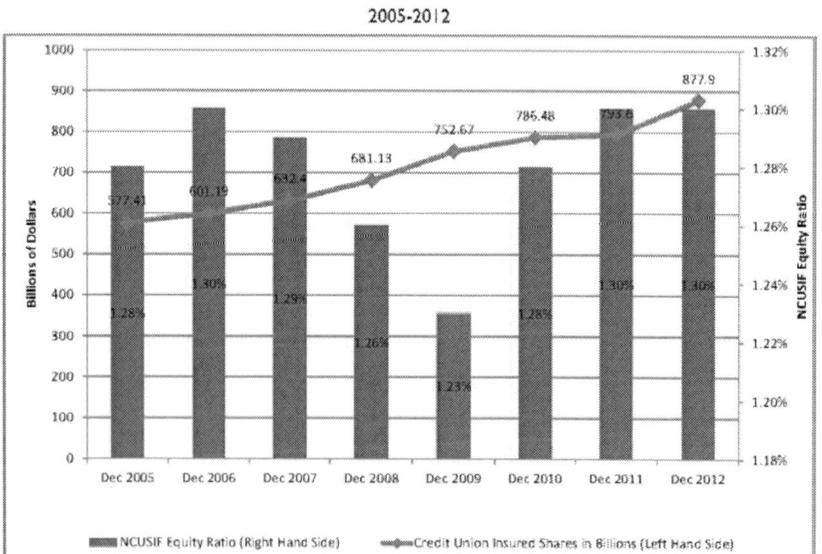

Source: NCUA.

Figure 3.Total NCUA-Insured Share Deposits and NCUSIF Equity Ratio.

2005-2012

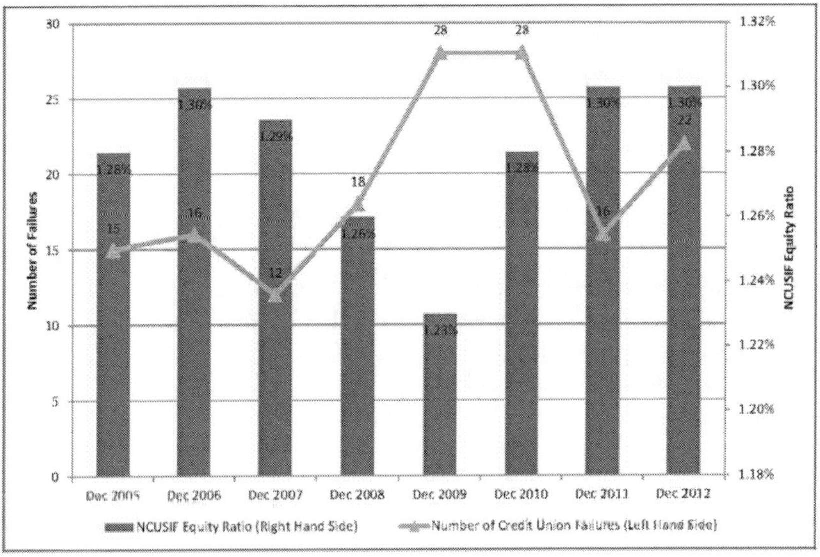

Source: NCUA.
Notes: Figures are annual or cumulative for the given year.

Figure 4. NCUSIF Equity Ratio and Annual Credit Union Failures.

During 2008, the NCUA chairman reported that corporate credit unions faced increasing liquidity pressures. A significant portion of their mortgage-backed securities had lost value and were downgraded below investment grade due to deterioration of the underlying collateral.[27] In March 2009, the NCUA placed two corporate credit unions, the U.S. Central Federal Credit Union and the Western Corporate Federal Credit Union, into conservatorship. In September 2010, Constitution Corporate Federal Credit Union, Members United Corporate Federal Credit Union, and Southwest Corporate Federal Credit Union were also placed into conservatorship. The chairman reported that the five corporates under conservatorship had represented approximately 70% of the entire corporate system's assets and 98.6% of the investment losses within the system.

At the end of 2012, there were $877.9 billion NCUA-insured share deposits and 22 credit union failures for the year.[28] **Figure 3** illustrates the total amount of NCUA-insured share deposits and the NCUSIF equity ratio. The NCUSIF equity ratio, which was 1.28% at the end of December 2005, was 1.30% as of December 31, 2012. **Figure 4** illustrates the NCUSIF equity ratio along with the number of credit union failures.[29] **Appendix B** discusses the

Temporary Corporate Credit Union Stabilization Fund (TCCUSF), which accounts for the corporate credit union losses, as well as other actions taken to minimize losses to the NCUSIF and the credit union system.

THE RESOLUTION PROCESS FOR INSOLVENT DEPOSITORY INSTITUTIONS

If an insured depository institution fails to maintain sufficient levels of capital or net worth to meet safety and soundness requirements, it is closed, and the assets of the institution are generally sold to another qualified depository institution. The FDIC and NCUA resolution procedures are described below.

Bank Failures and the FDIC

Bank assets include the consumer and commercial loans that banks originate and hold in portfolio; bank liabilities include the funds that banks borrow to provide loans to consumers and businesses. Whenever customers (depositors) make savings or checking deposits into a bank, the bank is effectively borrowing from them and using their funds to originate loans. A bank typically borrows the funds from its depositors for shorter periods of time with the expectation that these short-term borrowings must be continuously renewed until its longer-term loans held in portfolio have been fully repaid. For example, suppose a bank originates a consumer loan that a customer is expected to repay in full over two years. During those two years that the customer is borrowing, the bank will simultaneously “fund the loan,” meaning that it will treat its depositors’ funds as a sequence of quarterly (for a total of eight quarters) or monthly (for a total of 24 months) short-term loans and make periodic interest payments to depositors. In other words, banks (and credit unions) make loans to their customers for longer periods of time while they simultaneously borrow from their depositors in sequences of loans having shorter maturities.

Although banks may fund loans from creditors who are not depositors, deposits have traditionally been considered the most stable and inexpensive funding source, in particular for the smaller community banks, because depositors typically are the least sensitive to short-term interest rate fluctuations.[30] Nevertheless, banks can also borrow funds via participation in the federal funds market, by using repurchase agreements, by obtaining advances (loans) from the Federal Home Loan Bank System (FHLB); in addition, some of the larger banks may issue short-term commercial paper. Given that the short-term borrowings of a financial institution are refinanced more frequently, the composition of its liabilities (i.e., the ratio of deposit to non-deposit creditors) changes more frequently than the composition of its longer-term, less liquid assets (portfolio of loans). Hence, the total amounts of federally insured deposits are estimates at any point in time and are not known with certainty until an institution fails.[31]

A variety of financial ratios (e.g., total risk-based capital, tier 1 risk-based capital, tier 1 leverage, tangible equity ratios) are computed to determine whether a bank has sufficient reserves to act as buffers against default and liquidity risks.[32] If a bank's lending activities fail to generate enough income to maintain these buffers, then it will become insolvent.[33] A bank failing to meet the minimum required ratio thresholds would be considered insolvent, and its regulator (chartering authority and examiner) is likely to shut it down before the losses grow so large that it becomes unable to repay most of the principal and interest accruing to depositors. The regulator would also appoint the FDIC as the receiver of the failed institution.

As the receiver of a failed bank, the FDIC determines the resolution transaction that is least costly to the DIF by evaluating all possible resolution alternatives and then computing the costs on a net present value basis. The FDIC is required by law to pursue the least-costly transaction to minimize the impact on the DIF.[34] The least-costly transaction typically will involve some form of the purchase and assumption process, generally referred to as "P&A."[35] A P&A is a resolution transaction in which a healthy institution *purchases* some or all of the assets (outstanding loans) of a failed bank or thrift and assumes some or all of the *liabilities* (deposits).[36] The FDIC seeks bids from qualified institutions for the failed bank's assets.[37] The FDIC accepts the bid that is judged to be the least-costly option to the DIF and closes the failed bank. The transfers of assets and liabilities are typically completed over a weekend to minimize any disruptions to bank customers' access to their funds.

The total losses to the DIF may exceed any costs to reimburse depositors because additional costs associated with resolving a bank failure also apply. For example, some of the bank creditors may require repayment ahead of depositors. If a bank borrowed funds from the FHLB, the FDIC must repay the FHLB immediately because the FHLB's "super lien" status gives it priority over depositors.[38] In addition, the FDIC often provides assistance typically by entering into loss- sharing agreements with acquirers of a failed bank's assets. This assistance limits the amount of potential losses that may arise from loans transferred to an acquiring institution's balance sheet, which may threaten its solvency. Furthermore, any assets not purchased by an acquirer must still be liquidated by the FDIC.[39] Hence, the inability to know the amount of insured deposits until the bank failure occurs, when also considered with the additional costs associated with administration of the P&A process, increases the difficulty to predict the costs to the DIF.

Credit Union Failures and the NCUA

The NCUA, similar to the FDIC, uses a net worth-asset ratio to determine the solvency of a credit union.[40] The NCUA computes a credit union's net worth-asset ratio by dividing its net worth by its assets.[41] Under-capitalized credit unions, which typically have capital-asset ratios below the NCUA's minimum thresholds, would be considered insolvent.[42] If a credit union lacks sufficient net worth, the NCUA, which is often the primary federal regulator, will shut down the institution and then act as the receiver.

The NCUA, similar to the FDIC, is also required by law to pursue the least-costly transaction to minimize the impact on the NCUSIF of a failing credit union. The NCUA also employs a P&A process in which bids are obtained from qualified institutions for the assets of a failed credit union, and the accepted bid is the one judged to be the least-costly option to the NCUSIF.[43] The total losses to the NCUSIF, as in the case of bank failures, are not limited to any costs to reimburse insured share deposit holders. The NCUSIF would also absorb the administrative costs associated with resolving a credit union failure (i.e., repayment of FHLB loans that have priority over share depositors, loss sharing agreements entered with acquiring institutions, the liquidation of any remaining assets not purchased by acquirers).[44]

Insurance Fund(s) Insolvency and Taxpayer Risk

The risk to U.S. taxpayers to bear the losses of failed institutions increases when one or both of the insurance funds become depleted or insolvent. Insolvency of the insurance funds may occur after a systemic risk event (or an unexpected economic downturn or financial market collapse), which may generate numerous institutional failures. For example, a sudden decline in residential or commercial real estate values can cause the loan portfolios of numerous banks to deteriorate. In addition, an economic downturn that affects a particular industry or geographic area may be particularly devastating to the asset portfolios of smaller institutions. For instance, given their membership restrictions, credit unions with members consisting primarily of construction workers who experienced large job losses in the recent recession would be more likely to see a multitude of loan defaults.[45] Similarly, small banks or credit unions operating within a defined geographic region that experienced relatively large home value declines would see widespread mortgage defaults. Consequently, a sudden financial downturn that affects the portfolios of numerous depository institutions can drain deposit insurance funds just as quickly as the failure of a large financial institution. Hence, a systemic risk event, along with a procyclical bias in the pricing of deposit assessments (discussed in **Appendix A**), increases the risk of insurance fund insolvency.

Depletion of either or both deposit insurance funds may result in borrowings from the U.S. Treasury to protect depositors, with the taxpayer bearing the costs if those borrowings are not repaid. The DIF became insolvent by the third quarter of 2009, but the FDIC has been able to avoid having to borrow from the U.S. Treasury despite the numerous bank failures. On the other hand, the NCUSIF remained solvent; however, corporate credit union losses that may have been charged to the fund were placed onto an off-balance sheet account that has been funded by a line of credit from the U.S. Treasury. Consequently, the credit union system via the NCUA must repay the U.S. Treasury to prevent taxpayers from bearing any losses. The following appendixes discuss in more detail the efforts by legislators and the federal regulators to protect the DIF, NCUSIF, and ultimately, the taxpayers.

APPENDIX A. RECENT EFFORTS TO SUPPORT THE DEPOSIT INSURANCE FUND

As noted in **Figure 1** and **Figure 2**, the DIF began declining in 2008, and it became negative by the third quarter of 2009. The designated reserve ratio (DRR) was -0.16 during the third quarter of 2009, and reached a low of -0.39 during the fourth quarter of 2009. The DRR rose to 0.06 during the second quarter of 2011 and has so far remained positive. The decline in the DRR was due to both an increase in deposit insurance coverage during the crisis and the increase in bank failures. Congress and the FDIC took actions to support the DIF, which are discussed in this appendix.

Increase in FDIC Borrowing Authority

On February 3, 2009, the FDIC asked Congress to increase its line of credit from the U.S. Treasury to $100 billion from $30 billion.[46] The increased borrowing authority would be used in case funds from the DIF were not immediately available to meet the demands of rising bank closures.[47] HFSTHA temporarily increased the FDIC's borrowing authority from $30 billion to $500 billion until December 31, 2010; as of January 1, 2011, the FDIC has $100 billion of permanent borrowing authority from the U.S. Treasury.[48]

Elimination of a Procyclical Bias in Deposit Insurance Pricing

The Federal Deposit Insurance Corporation Improvement Act of 1991 (FDICIA) granted the FDIC authority to implement a risk-based assessment system, which was implemented on January 1, 1993.[49] Under a risk-based assessment system, financial institutions that pose more risk to the DIF are assessed higher deposit insurance premiums relative to those that pose lower risk. The Deposit Insurance Funds Act of 1996, however, mandated that institutions that are both well-capitalized and have received high examination ratings shall not be charged premiums when the DIF is at or above the statutorily set DRR.[50] Some economists have argued that this limitation injected a procyclical bias into the pricing of deposit insurance.[51] In other words, the DIF would not be permitted to accumulate reserves in excess of the DRR during financially stable periods; consequently, deposit premiums may increase dramatically during a financial downturn, when it is more difficult for banks to pay higher assessments while maintaining sufficient profitability.

In 2001, FDIC Chair Donna Tanoue testified that this statutory provision resulted in 92% of insured depository institutions in the FDIC's best-risk category not having to pay deposit insurance assessments, which rendered its risk-based premium system ineffective.[52] For this reason, the FDIC requested elimination of the statutory restrictions on its ability to charge risk- based premiums to all institutions even when the DIF level exceeds its statutory requirement. On February 8, 2006, the Federal Deposit Insurance Reform Act of 2005 (Reform Act; P.L. 109-171) was signed by the President into law, giving the FDIC the authority to charge premiums to individual banks, after notice and comment rulemaking, based upon the riskiness of the institutions, regardless of the level of the DRR.[53] On July 16, 2006, the FDIC then proposed new risk-based deposit premium assessments, which were approved on November 2, 2006.[54] The FDIC was still unable to collect assessments, however, when the DIF exceeded 1.35% at the end of a calendar year. Given that the Reform Act requires the FDIC to rebate excess assessments in the form of dividends to financial institutions, a procyclical bias in the pricing of deposit assessments apparently remained.[55]

The Dodd-Frank Act eliminates procyclical deposit insurance assessments by giving the FDIC sole discretion to suspend or limit the declaration of the payment of dividends to financial institutions.[56] This provision allows the FDIC to continue collecting assessments regardless of the DRR level. This authority in principle enhances the effectiveness of a risk-based assessment system (discussed below) designed to encourage prudent lending practices. Furthermore, the FDIC announced on December 20, 2010, that it would pursue a DRR of 2% as a minimum level to reduce the risk that the DIF would become negative in a future crisis similar to the magnitude of the most recent crisis.[57]

Changes to the Pricing of Deposit Insurance

On April 8, 2010, the FDIC announced proposed revisions to the current system of determining assessments via a Notice of Proposed Rulemaking (NPR) on Assessments.[58] On November 10, 2010, the FDIC made further revisions to the system in light of the Dodd-Frank Act.[59] On February 7, 2011, the FDIC approved a final rule on assessments, dividends, the assessment base, and the pricing of deposit insurance for large banks, with an effective date of April 1, 2011.[60] The new system takes a formal risk analysis approach, similar to methodologies used in credit underwriting.[61] This approach attempts to more accurately capture risk at the time the institution assumes the risk and, therefore, to better predict when an institution's risk profile may change.[62]

The assessment system has separate assessment structures for large depository institutions, highly complex institutions, and small depository institutions, respectively. A large depository institution is defined as one having $10 billion or more in total assets for at least four consecutive quarters. A highly complex institution is defined as a depository institution with more than $50 billion in total assets that is fully owned by a parent company with more than $500 billion in total assets (or fully owned by one or more intermediate parent companies with more than $500 billion in assets), or a processing bank and trust company with more than $10 billion in total assets.[63] Small institutions, which do not fit into the other categories, are assessed separately.

Data for the large depository institutions and the highly complex institutions,[64] which are collected during examinations, are evaluated using a scorecard with variables from the following categories:

- a weighted average CAMELS[65] rating;
- variables that represent the ability to withstand a decline in asset holdings or an increase in credit or default risk, such as risk-based capital-to-asset ratios;
- variables that represent the ability to withstand an increase in liquidity or funding risk, such as the ratio of core deposits to total liabilities; and
- a loss severity score that measures the relative magnitude of potential losses to the FDIC, which is computed as a ratio of possible losses to the total domestic deposits, averaged over three quarters.

After the data have been entered, the scorecard would compute a performance score and a loss severity score between 0 and 100. The performance and the loss severity scores would then be converted to an *initial* base assessment rate. The *final* assessment rate would then be computed by adjusting the initial base assessment rate for holdings of certain long-term unsecured debt, secured liabilities, and brokered deposits. Use of the scorecard allows assessments to vary with the levels of risk taken by institutions each quarter. Consequently, this system may provide incentives to institutions to reduce excessive risks, in particular during economic expansions when loan underwriting standards tend to be relatively more relaxed.

For small depository institutions, a risk-based deposit insurance assessment is still calculated based primarily upon their CAMELS ratings and capitalization levels. Financial institutions receive a composite CAMELS rating from 1 to 5, with 1 being the most favorable rating of an institution's overall condition and performance. Next, they are assigned capitalization classifications, which are determined by their various leverage ratios: "Well capitalized," "Adequately capitalized," "Undercapitalized," "Significantly undercapitalized," and "Critically undercapitalized." The institutions can now be grouped into four risk categories:

- Risk Category I (Well capitalized and with CAMELS ratings of 1 or 2);
- Risk Category II (Adequately capitalized and with CAMELS ratings of 2 or 3);
- Risk Category III (Undercapitalized with higher CAMELS ratings or currently not undercapitalized with CAMELS ratings of 4 or 5); or
- Risk Category IV (all other undercapitalized institutions).

The final assessment rate for each of the risk categories is computed using a predetermined initial base assessment rate followed by adjustments made based upon the bank's holdings of unsecured debt, secured liabilities, and brokered deposits.

With passage of the Dodd-Frank Act, the assessment base is now defined as the average total consolidated assets during the assessment period minus *the sum* of (1) the average tangible equity and (2) any additional amount the FDIC determines is necessary to reflect risks posed by certain financial institutions such as custodial banks.[66] Under the previous assessment structure, banks may have been able to select non-deposit short-term funding options, thus reducing the amount of deposit insurance assessments they would have to pay. With an expanded assessment base, deposit premiums for the DIF would be collected regardless of the funding strategies pursued. The additional funds could potentially cover more of the additional costs that must be incurred to resolve a bank failure.

Increase in Deposit Insurance Assessments

On October 7, 2008 (with a DRR at 0.76 for the third quarter), the FDIC announced a plan to restore the DIF to its statutory requirement by the end of 2013.[67] Under the plan, deposit insurance assessments increased by seven basis points (or 0.07 percentage points) beginning January 1, 2009. The FDIC announced modifications to its original restoration plan on February 27, 2009.[68] The time horizon deemed necessary to accumulate the DRR level for the DIF was extended to seven years from the initial five. In the February 27, 2009, announcement, the FDIC also imposed a special assessment fee on all banks to help replenish the DIF. The FDIC also imposed an emergency special assessment of 5 basis points (0.05%) on member banks on June 30, 2009, to be collected on September 30, 2009.[69] Hence, the FDIC's response during the banking crisis appears to have been consistent with academics' earlier warnings of a procyclical bias in the deposit assessment pricing system.

Prepaid Insurance Assessments

On November 12, 2009, the FDIC approved a final rule requiring its member institutions to prepay deposit insurance assessments covering all of 2010, 2011, and 2012, to be collected on December 30, 2009, along with the regular assessments due for the fourth quarter of 2009.[70] The assessment *rate* was calculated using the institution's rate as of September 30, 2009, and the rate applied to 2011 and 2012 was 3 basis points (0.03%) higher. The assessment *base* or amount of deposits was calculated using the institution's third quarter assessment base, and the base was estimated to grow at 5% annually through the end of 2012. The FDIC announced that it would consider requests to be exempted from the prepayment requirement on a case-by-case basis.[71]

The FDIC has other options for reducing its liquidity needs. The FDIC could impose additional special assessments or exercise its authority to borrow from the U.S. Treasury or the Federal Financing Bank. These options would still result in higher assessments on member institutions. According to the FDIC, member institutions would repay such borrowings through assessments. Consequently, member institutions will pay either today or in the future to restore the DIF. The prepayment option arguably would be less expensive for the industry than borrowing from the Treasury today and repaying later with additional interest charges. Paying more for deposit insurance could, however, be burdensome for some member institutions, in particular during a period of financial uncertainty when loan defaults may increase and earnings from lending activities decrease.

Temporary Liquidity Guarantee Program

On October 14, 2008, the FDIC created the Temporary Liquidity Guarantee Program (TLGP) to encourage liquidity in the banking system.[72] One component of the program guarantees senior unsecured debt issued before October 31, 2009.[73] Such debt structures include commercial paper, interbank funding debt, promissory notes, and any unsecured portion of secured debt. The guarantee remained in effect until June 30, 2012.

Also, a surcharge was imposed on any debt issued on or after April 1, 2009, with a maturity date of one year or more.[74] The Transaction Account Guarantee (TAG) component insured all non-interest-bearing deposit accounts, primarily payroll processing accounts used by businesses, which often exceed the $250,000 deposit insurance limit.[75]

Financial institutions eligible for participation in the TLGP program include entities insured by the FDIC, bank holding and financial holding companies headquartered in the United States, and savings and loan companies under Section 4(k) of the Bank Holding Company Act of 1956. Although the TLGP was a voluntary program, eligible financial institutions were automatically registered to participate unless they had requested to be excluded by November 12, 2008. Eligible entities could also opt out of one or both of the program components.

After the first 30 days, institutions that remained in the program paid insurance fees.[76] To insure senior unsecured debt, the FDIC assessed an annualized fee corresponding to 75 basis points. A 10-basis-point surcharge was applied for non-interest-bearing deposit accounts above the $250,000 deposit insurance limit. According to testimony by the FDIC's deputy to the chairman, almost 7,000 of 8,300 FDIC-insured institutions opted in to the transaction account guarantee program, and nearly 7,100 banks and their holding companies opted into the debt guarantee program.[77]

On April 13, 2010, the FDIC adopted a final rule extending the TAG portion of the TLGP for six months through December 31, 2010.[78] After passage of the Dodd-Frank Act, participation in TAG became mandatory for all insured depository institutions, and the unlimited insurance for their non-interest bearing accounts was extended for two years beginning December 31, 2010.[79] TAG was allowed to expire on December 31, 2012.

The FDIC has reported that losses from the TAG program to date have not been large enough to materially affect the goal to reach the statutory DIF reserve ratio (the DRR) requirement of 1.35 by September 30, 2020.[80] The TAG deposits represented a small percentage of failed bank deposits because a greater share of them was held in larger institutions.[81] Now that the TAG program has expired, TAG deposits are no longer used in the calculation of the DRR, which arguably moves the ratio more quickly toward its statutory requirement.

Appendix B. Recent Efforts to Support the NCUSIF

As noted in **Figure 3** and **Figure 4**, the NCUSIF began to decline after 2006. The 2006 equity ratio was 1.30% and fell to 1.18% by August 2010, which was below the statutory minimum of 1.2%. Congress and the NCUA took actions to support the NCUSIF, which are discussed in this appendix.

Temporary Corporate Credit Union Stabilization Fund

HFSTHA established the Temporary Corporate Credit Union Stabilization Fund (TCCUSF, or the Stabilization Fund) to absorb losses related to the corporate credit union investments. The NCUA may borrow from the Stabilization Fund, which is a line of credit provided by the U.S. Treasury for a seven-year period, to pay only for the expenditures associated with conservatorship or a liquidation of a corporate credit union.[82] In addition, HFSTHA raised the NCUA borrowing authority from the U.S. Treasury from $100 million to $6 billion as well as emergency borrowing up to $30 billion.[83] The aggregate total is available to both the NCUSIF and the TCCUSF. The NCUA is responsible for imposing premium assessments on federally insured credit unions to repay the Treasury in seven years.[84]

Enhancement of the Central Liquidity Facility

The Central Liquidity Facility (CLF) is a mixed-ownership U.S. government corporation that Congress created in 1978 to provide a source of seasonal and emergency liquidity for credit unions.[85] The CLF exists within the NCUA and is owned by member credit unions. Credit unions, however, are encouraged not to rely upon the CLF as a conventional funding or liquidity source; instead, it should be used as a back-up source of funds, similar in manner to the Federal Reserve System's discount window. Congress raised the CLF's borrowing cap from $1.5 billion to its full statutory limit of $41 billion.[86]

The National Credit Union Authority Clarification Act of 2010

The National Credit Union Authority Clarification Act of 2010 (NCUACA; P.L. 111-382, 124 Stat. 4134) made the following statutory changes that would help reduce losses to the NCUSIF:[87]

- Changes in accounting definitions and standards, which are made by the Financial Accounting Standard Board (FASB), may indirectly affect the NCUSIF when its loans and account ledger definitions must remain the same by statute.[88] For example, the net worth of a healthy or surviving credit union would be diluted after a merger with a troubled credit union, given that the statutory definition of "net worth" did not treat NCUA assistance as capital. Consequently, the NCUA had to liquidate a failed credit union rather than arrange for a merger with a healthier credit union, and such liquidation may have been a more costly option for the NCUSIF.[89] NCUACA gives the NCUA Board the authority to modify accounting definitions as accounting standards change, thus creating another viable and less costly option for resolving a failed institution.
- NCUACA clarified the definition of the NCUSIF equity ratio. Given that credit unions must maintain 1% of their deposits in the NCUSIF, a recent change in accounting standards concerning mergers may have resulted in the consolidation of the NCUSIF financial statements with those of the participating credit unions. Consequently, the equity ratio would likely fall below its statutory limit and thus trigger additional mandatory premium assessments to re-capitalize the NCUSIF if it were computed using a consolidated balance sheet, which would also include the Stabilization Fund and any credit unions under conservatorship. The amendment, therefore, states that the equity ratio is based solely upon the unconsolidated financial statements of the NCUSIF. This amendment also gives the NCUA more flexibility in terms of when and how much assessments should rise so that repayment of the Stabilization Fund does not become too burdensome on the credit union system.
- Prior to NCUACA, the Stabilization Fund had to borrow from the U.S. Treasury to manage losses in the corporate credit union system. This eliminated the option to raise premiums on credit unions until after a debt obligation to Treasury had been incurred. The credit union system must repay both the costs associated with the failures and

interest costs when it borrows from Treasury. The ability to raise premiums on the credit union system to repay losses without having to incur additional borrowing costs, therefore, may be less burdensome.[90]

NCUA Restructuring of Corporate Credit Union Regulatory Framework

On September 24, 2010, NCUA issued final amendments to its rule governing corporate credit unions.[91] Among the numerous revisions, corporate credit unions will now be regulated for safety and soundness under a risk-based capital scheme similar to FDIC insured banks. Rather than just a single capital ratio, the corporates must now meet three minimum capital ratios—a leverage ratio, a tier 1 risk-based capital ratio, and a total risk-based capital ratio.[92] The new capital requirements would be phased in over a 10-year period. In addition, prompt corrective actions will now apply to corporates that fail to meet the capital requirements. A prompt corrective action may include restrictions on activities, investments, payment of dividends, restrictions on executive compensation, requirements to dismiss management and elect new directors, and possible conservatorship.

Increase in NCUSIF Premium Assessments

On September 16, 2010, the NCUA approved a share deposit premium charge of 12.42 basis points (or 0.1242 percentage points) of insured shares.[93] When combined with the premium charge for the Stabilization Fund, the total premium being charged to credit unions is 26 basis points. The premium assessment reflected a plan to restore the NCUSIF equity ratio to 1.3%, which happened by December 2011.

Temporary Guarantees

The U.S. Central Federal Credit Union provided services to the other corporate credit unions. The NCUA infused $1 billion into the U.S. Central Federal Credit Union by issuing a NCUSIF capital note and implementing a temporary guarantee on uninsured shares on deposit at corporate credit unions.[94] The purpose of this action was to maintain external sources of funding in the institution by preserving the confidence of creditors.

Similar to the FDIC's TLGP and TAG programs, the NCUA also established voluntary guarantee programs.[95] For example, the Temporary Corporate Credit Union Liquidity Guarantee Program (TCCULGP), which is analogous to TLGP, was approved by NCUA on October 16, 2008.[96] Under TCCULGP, the NCUF provided a 100% guarantee on new unsecured debt obligations issued by eligible corporate credit unions on or before June 30, 2009, and maturing on or before June 30, 2010. These unsecured obligations included promissory notes, commercial paper, and inter-bank funding, and any unsecured portion of secured debt.

Similar to the FDIC's TAG, the Temporary Corporate Credit Union Share Guarantee Program (TCCUSGP) guaranteed the uninsured shares of corporate credit unions (shares owned by the retail credit unions that exceed the NCUSIF insurance limits) through December 31, 2010.[97] After passage of the Dodd-Frank Act, TCCUSGP was extended through December 31, 2012.[98]

End Notes

[1] See http://www2.fdic.gov/qbp/2009dec/qbp.pdf.

[2] See NCUSIF and TCCUSF Statistics, http://www.ncua.gov/Resources/Reports/ncusif/2011/2011JuneBoardSlides.pdf.

[3] 48 Stat. 162, 12 U.S.C. See Christine Bradley, "A Historical Perspective on Deposit Insurance," Federal Deposit Insurance Corporation, *FDIC Banking Review*, December 2000, p. 3, http://www.fdic.gov/bank/analytical/banking/ 2000dec/brv13n2_1.pdf.

[4] P.L. 111-203, Section 627 repeals the prohibition of payment of interest on demand deposit accounts beginning one year after enactment. The FDIC also insures Money Market Deposit Accounts, which are savings accounts that allow a limited number of checks to be written each month; Negotiable Orders of Withdrawal (NOW) accounts; and outstanding cashiers' checks.

[5] The FDIC also insures the following retirement accounts: Keogh retirement accounts for the self-employed, 457 Plan retirement accounts for state government employees, and employer-sponsored defined contribution plan retirement accounts that are self-directed, which are primarily 401(k) accounts and include SIMPLE 401(k) accounts, Simplified Employee Pension (SEP) IRAs, and Savings Incentive Match Plans for Employees (SIMPLE) IRAs.

[6] The FDIC does not insure stocks, bonds, mutual funds, money market funds, life insurance policies, annuities, or municipal securities, even if these products were purchased from an insured bank. The FDIC does not insure the contents of safe deposit boxes, losses due to theft or fraud at the bank, losses due to accounting errors, and investments backed by the U.S. government, such as Treasury securities and Savings Bonds. See Federal Deposit Insurance Corporation, "One-Stop Shopping for Financial Services: A Window of Opportunity for the Informed Consumer," *FDIC Consumer News–Spring 2001*, FDIC, 2001, http://www.fdic.gov/CONSUMERS/consumer/news/cnspr01/ cvrstry.html.

[7] FDIC, "Fall 2008–Special Edition: Your New, Higher FDIC Insurance Coverage," *FDIC Consumer News*, 2008, http://www.fdic.gov/consumers

[8] In addition to deposit insurance coverage, the FDIC announced the creation of the Temporary Liquidity Guarantee Program on October 14, 2008, to encourage liquidity in the banking system. One component of the program guarantees senior unsecured debt issued by depository institutions. The Transaction Account Guarantee component insures payroll processing accounts used by businesses, which are non-interest bearing deposit accounts. See **Appendix A**.

[9] P.L. 109-171, 110 Stat. 9.

[10] See also CRS Report RL34730, *Troubled Asset Relief Program: Legislation and Treasury Implementation*, by Baird Webel and Edward V. Murphy.

[11] P.L. 111-22, 123 Stat. 1632, Section 204.

[12] P.L. 111-203, 124 Stat. 1376, Sec. 335. The increase in deposit insurance was also made retroactive to cover funds for depositors that were uninsured in the six institutions for which the FDIC was appointed receiver or conservator after January 1, 2008. See announcement at http://www.fdic.gov/news/news/press/2010/pr10162.html. For a brief summary of changes relevant to the FDIC after passage of the Dodd-Frank Act, see http://www.fdic.gov/regulations/reform/ summary.html or CRS Report R41339, *The Dodd-Frank Wall Street Reform and Consumer Protection Act: Titles III and VI, Regulation of Depository Institutions and Depository Institution Holding Companies*, by M. Maureen Murphy.

[13] See "Final Rule on Special Assessment" at http://www.fdic.gov/news/board/May22no2.pdf.

[14] P.L. 111-203, Sec. 334.

[15] See FDIC *Quarterly Banking Report* as of December 31, 2012, at http://www2.fdic.gov/qbp/2012dec/qbp.pdf.

[16] Large losses to the DIF have come from failures of such institutions as IndyMac Bank, Downey Savings and Loan, PFF Bank and Trust, Franklin Bank, and First National Bank of Nevada. For the FDIC's complete Failed Bank List, see http://www.fdic.gov/bank/individual/failed/banklist.html. For a brief description of each bank failure, see http://www.fdic.gov/BANK/HISTORICAL/BANK/index.html.

[17] See FDIC's 2012 Annual Performance Plan at http://www.fdic.gov/about/strategic/performance/insurance.html.

[18] For additional information about the credit unions along with comparisons to banks, see CRS Report R42574, *Credit Union Commercial Business Lending: Key Issues for Legislation in the 112th Congress*, by Darryl E. Getter.

[19] The Federal Credit Union Act of 1934 (48 Stat. 1216). P.L. 91-468, 84 Stat. 994 made the NCUA an independent agency, which is governed by a three-member Board.

[20] Prior to passage of the Dodd-Frank Act, the Office of Thrift Supervision chartered and supervised thrift institutions. After Dodd-Frank, thrifts are now supervised by the Office of the Comptroller of the Currency. The Federal Reserve also provides payment settlement services to financial institutions. See http://www.kansascityfed.org/publicat/PSR/Briefings/PSR-BriefingAug06.pdf.

[21] State regulators have primary supervisory authority over state-chartered credit unions that are federally insured. Given that federal deposit insurance is optional in some states, some state-chartered credit unions are privately insured by American Share Insurance, which means the share deposits are not backed by the full faith and credit of the U.S. government. See http://www.americanshare.com/Public/Home.aspx.

[22] See http://www.ncua.gov/DataApps/Pages/SI-FAQs.aspx.

[23] The insurance coverage for eligible retirement accounts was raised by two laws passed in the 109th Congress, P.L. 109-171, 120 Stat. 4 and P.L. 109-173, 119 Stat. 3601; see 12 U.S.C. 1781-1790d.

[24] July 18, 1984, 98 Stat. 494. The 1% is carried on each individual institution's books as an asset.

[25] The Federal Credit Union Act (12 USC 1782(h)(4)). See http://www.house.gov/apps/list/hearing/financialsvcs_dem/ bedinger_-_nafcu.pdf.

[26] In this context, a procyclical bias exists when the collection of assessments is tied to the size of the insurance fund, thus increasing the correlation between the insurance fund's solvency risk and the level of distress experienced by the insured depository institutions. Under a procyclical bias, credit unions would also be more likely see an increase in share deposit insurance premiums during economic downturns when it is more difficult to maintain profitability. The Dodd-Frank Act eliminated the procyclical bias with respect to the pricing of FDIC deposit insurance assessments, but the procyclical bias still exists with the pricing of NCUA deposit insurance assessments. For more information on this issue as it related to the FDIC, see **Appendix A**.

[27] See Statement of Deborah Matz, chairman, National Credit Union Administration, "The State of the Credit Union Industry," p. 3, at http://www.ncua.gov/News/Documents/SP20101209Matz.pdf, which was given in U.S. Congress, Senate Committee on Banking, Housing, and Urban Affairs, 111th Cong., 2nd sess., December 9, 2010.

[28] See http://www.ncua.gov/Legal/Documents/Reports/IAG201212.pdf.

[29] See http://www.ncua.gov/Legal/Documents/Reports/SI-Slides201212.pdf. The NCUSIF's equity ratio does not reflect the total losses to the credit union system, given that it does not account for the corporate credit union conservatorships.

[30] The cost to fund bank assets with deposits increases when households shift from holding assets in the form of bank deposits to non-bank investment vehicles, which may offer higher returns, or when deposit insurance premiums increase. For more information on the decline of core deposits and the impact on small banks, see http://www.kansascityfed.org/banking

[31] See Andrew M. Davenport, Joseph V. Fellerman, and Lynn Shibut et al., "An Evaluation of the Denominator of the Reserve Ratio," Federal Deposit Insurance Corporation, *FDIC Staff Study*, February 12, 2007, http://www.fdic.gov/deposit/insurance/initiative/ Denominator _Board.pdf.

[32] For more information on bank regulatory capital and liquidity ratios, see CRS Report R42744, *U.S. Implementation of the Basel Capital Regulatory Framework*, by Darryl E. Getter.

[33] Note that a bank does not have to be insolvent to be illiquid. A bank can hold more of its assets in the form of loans as opposed to cash. If, however, those assets cannot quickly be turned into cash, the bank may face cash flow problems if there is an unusual demand for cash by depositors.

[34] See Statement of Mitchell L. Glassman, director of the Division of Resolutions and Receiverships at the FDIC on the Condition of Financial Institutions: Examining the Failure and Seizure of an American Bank before the Subcommittee on Financial Institutions and Consumer Credit; House Committee on Financial Services, January 21, 2010, at http://www.fdic.gov/news/news/speeches/chairman/spjan2110.html.

[35] Although the FDIC has various resolution options and chooses the least costly one, the P&A process is the most frequently used option. See CRS Report RL34657, *Financial Institution Insolvency: Federal Authority over Fannie Mae, Freddie Mac, and Depository Institutions*, by David H. Carpenter and M. Maureen Murphy; Federal Deposit Insurance Corporation, *Managing the Crisis: The FDIC and RTC Experience 1980-1994* (Washington, DC: Federal Deposit Insurance Corporation, 1998) at http://www.fdic.gov/bank/historical/managing/contents.pdf; and http://www.fdic.gov/bank/historical/managing/history1-02.pdf for more details regarding the resolution process.

[36] See Chapter 3 of the FDIC's *Resolution Handbook* at http://www.fdic.gov/bank/historical/reshandbook/ch3pas.pdf.

[37] Qualified institutions are those that obtain approval from their chartering authorities. See http://www.fdic.gov/buying/financial/index.html for more information about the qualification process for financial institutions wanting to participate in an FDIC asset sale.

[38] For more information about the FHLB's super lien status, see http://www.fdic.gov/about/learn/advisorycommittee/fhlb_advances.html, http://www.fdic.gov/about/learn/ advisory

committee/minutes111903.html, and CRS Report R41102, *The Federal Home Loan Bank System and Resolution of a Failure*, by N. Eric Weiss and Todd Garvey. For information on the National Depositor Preference Law, which stipulates the priority of payment structure that the FDIC must follow to resolve depository failures, see http://www.clevelandfed.org/Research/commentary/1994/0215.pdf. The FHLB may also assess prepayment fees that might be costly to the DIF when resolving a bank failure.

39 For information regarding some of the unusual bank assets that the FDIC has had to liquidate after various bank failures, see http://www.fdic.gov/bank/historical/managing/Chron/1933-79/.

40 The difference between assets minus liabilities is referred to as "capital" in connection with banks, which issue preferred and common equity shares. For credit unions, the difference between assets minus liabilities is referred to as "net worth" given that they do not issue equity shares.

41 The assets are also assigned risk-weights prior to computation of the net worth ratio.

42 For a table that summarizes the net worth-asset ratios used to evaluate safety and soundness compliance of NCUA insured credit, See Table 1—Statutory Net Worth Category Classification at http://www.ncua.gov/resources/ RegulationsOpinionsLaws/rules_and_regs/NCUA%20R%20&%20R%20Book%201%20May%208%202008.pdf.

43 See http://www.ncua.gov/letters/2010/CU/10-CU-11.pdf for more details regarding the NCUA's P&A process.

44 On November 17, 2010, the NCUA authorized the creation of a loss share pilot program to facilitate the resolution of large credit unions, based upon the FDIC's use of loss share agreements, to minimize losses to the NCUSIF. See http://www.ncua.gov/news/press_releases/2010/MA10-1117NCUAInitiatesPilotLossShareProgram.pdf.

45 For additional information on large job losses during the recent recession, see CRS Report R41434, *Job Growth During the Recovery*, by Linda Levine.

46 See Statement of John F. Bovenzi, deputy to the chairman and chief operating officer, FDIC on Promoting Bank Liquidity and Lending Through Deposit Insurance, Hope for Homeowners, and Other Enhancements before the Committee on Financial Services; U.S. House of Representatives, February 3, 2009, at http://www.fdic.gov/news/news/ speeches/archives/2009/spfeb0309.html.

47 For more detailed information concerning FDIC authority, see CRS Report RL34657, *Financial Institution Insolvency: Federal Authority over Fannie Mae, Freddie Mac, and Depository Institutions*, by David H. Carpenter and M. Maureen Murphy.

48 P.L. 111-22, 123 Stat. 1632, Section 204.

49 P.L. 102-242, 105 Stat. 2236 See "Assessment Rate Cases" at http://www.fdic.gov/deposit/insurance/assessments/ rate_cases.html.

50 P.L. 104-208, 110 Stat. 3009.

51 See Alan S. Blinder and Robert F. Wescott, *Reform of Deposit Insurance: A Report to the FDIC*, March 20, 2001, available at http://www.fdic.gov/deposit/insurance/initiative/ reform

52 See http://www.house.gov/financialservices/mediainitiative/direcommendations.html#ReCurrent, and http://www.frbsf.org/ publications/ economics/letter/2002/el2002- 14.html.

53 See http://www.fdic.gov/deposit/insurance/initiative/index.html for highlights regarding coverage of the law and a link to the Reform Act.

54 See "FDIC Proposes New Risk-Based Insurance Assessment System" at http://www.fdic.gov/news/news/press/2006/ pr06070.html and "FDIC Approves New Risk-Based Premiums for Deposit Insurance" at http://www.fdic.gov/news/ news/press/2006/pr06101.html.

55 See "Assessment Dividends" at http://www.fdic.gov/deposit/insurance/reform.html#drr.

56 P.L. 111-203, 124 Stat. 1376, Section 332.

57 For more information regarding the elimination of the procyclicality in the existing risk-based assessment system, see "Designated Reserve Ratio" at https://www.federalregister.gov/

articles/2010/12/20/2010-31829/designated-reserve- ratio and http://www.gpo.gov/fdsys/pkg/FR-2010-12-20/pdf/2010-31829.pdf.

[58] See Financial Institutions Letter (FIL-14-2010) at http://www.fdic.gov/news/news/ financialthe Federal Register at http://www.fdic.gov/regulationsand other links at http://www.fdic.gov/deposit/insurance/new.html, http://www.fdic.gov/news /board/april05.pdf, and http://www.fdic.gov/ news/board/april06.pdf. The comment period for the proposed rule ended on July 2, 2010.

[59] See Financial Institutions Letter (FIL-77-2010) at http://www.fdic.gov/news/news/financialand the Federal Register at http://www.fdic.gov/deposit/ insurance/2010-29137.pdf for more details.

[60] See Financial Institutions Letter (FIL-8-2011) at http://www.fdic.gov/news/news/financialand http://www.fdic.gov/news/news/press/2011/pr11028.html.

[61] See John W. Straka, "A Shift in the Mortgage Landscape: The 1990s Move to Automated Credit Evaluations," *Journal of Housing Research*, vol. 11, no. 2 (2000), pp. 207-232.

[62] The FDIC provides a complete description of the assessment system at http://www.fdic.gov/deposit/insurance/ 11RuleAD35.pdf.

[63] For a more precise definition of a highly complex institution, see http://www.fdic.gov/news/board/april05.pdf.

[64] A scorecard refers to scoring models and statistical automated methods used to assess the credit risk of individuals or entities based upon various characteristics. For example, the mortgage industry uses scorecards to categorize mortgage applicants into risk groups and set mortgage rates and terms. See John W. Straka, "A Shift in the Mortgage Landscape: The 1990s Move to Automated Credit Evaluations."

[65] The CAMELS rating assesses six components: Capital adequacy, Asset quality, Management administration, Earnings, Liquidity, and Sensitivity to market risk. See http://www.federalreserve.gov/boarddocs/press/general/1996/ 19961224/default.htm.

[66] P.L. 111-203, 124 Stat. 1376, Sec. 331. See Financial Institutions Letter (FIL-78-2010) at http://www.fdic.gov/news/ news/financial/2010/fil10078.html, which defines the assessment base as "average consolidated total assets minus average tangible equity," as required by the Dodd-Frank Act.

[67] See "FDIC Board Adopts Restoration Plan—Proposes Higher Assessments on Insured Banks" at http://www.fdic.gov/news/news/press/2008/pr08094.html.

[68] See "FDIC Extends Restoration Plan; Imposes Special Assessment" at http://www.fdic.gov/news/news/press/2009/ pr09030.html.

[69] See "Final Rule on Special Assessment" at http://www.fdic.gov/news/board/May22no2.pdf, which is a link to the memorandum to the FDIC Board of Directors, and also http://www.fdic.gov/news/board/May22no1.pdf for the official announcement of the final rule in the *Federal Register*.

[70] See http://www.fdic.gov/news/board/2009nov12no4.pdf for the official announcement of the final rule in the *Federal Register*

[71] See "FDIC Board Approves Final Rule on Prepaid Assessments" http://www.fdic.gov/news/news/press/2009/pr09203.html.

[72] See the initial announcement at http://www.fdic.gov/news/news/press/2008/pr08100.html. See http://www.fdic.gov/ news/news/press/2008/pr08105.html, which provides further details of the program.

[73] On March 17, 2009, the FDIC extended the original deadline from June 30, 2009, to October 31, 2009.

[74] See http://www.fdic.gov/news/news/press/2009/pr09041.html. Monthly reports on debt issuance under the TLGP program may be found at http://www.fdic.gov/regulations

[75] P.L. 111-203, 124 Stat. 1376, Section 627 repeals the prohibition of payment of interest on demand deposit accounts beginning one year after enactment.

[76] The list of institutions requesting not to participate in the TLGP program is available at http://www.fdic.gov/ regulations/resources/TLGP/optout.html.

[77] Statement of John F. Bovenzi, deputy to the chairman and chief operating officer, Federal Deposit Insurance Corporation, "Promoting Bank Liquidity and Lending Through Deposit Insurance, Hope for Homeowners, and Other Enhancements before the Committee on Financial Services," before U.S. House of Representatives, February 3, 2009, http://www.fdic.gov/news/news/speeches/archives/2009/spfeb0309.html.

[78] See CRS Report R42787, *An Overview of the Transaction Account Guarantee (TAG) Program and the Potential Impact of Its Expiration or Extension*, by Sean M. Hoskins; and http://www.fdic.gov/news/news/financial/2010/ fil10015.html.

[79] P.L. 111-203, 124 Stat. 1376, Section 343.

[80] See Letter from Martin J. Gruenberg, FDIC acting chairman, to Honorable Shelley Moore Capito, chairman, Subcommittee on Financial Institutions and Consumer Credit, Committee on Financial Services, House of Representatives, June 29, 2012, http://www.aba.com/Issues/Index/Documents/FDICResponsetoCapitoonTAG.pdf.

[81] Ibid. Banks that failed since the existence of the TAG programs had an average asset size below $1 billion. TAG costs were approximately 3% of the estimated total costs of bank failures under the original TAG program that ended in 2010 and approximately 3% to date under the extended TAG program.

[82] See http://www.ncua.gov/Resources/OIG/Files/Reports/2010/OIG-10-13FY2009 FSATCC USF.pdf.

[83] See http://www.ncua.gov/Resources/CorporateCU/Files/CULetters/09-CU-14Corp Stabiliza tionFundImplementation.pdf.

[84] See Board Action Bulletin, May 20, 2010, at http://www.ncua.gov/GenInfo/BoardandAction/reports/2010/BAB10- 0520.pdf.

[85] P.L. 95-630, 92 Stat. 3641. For additional information on the Central Liquidity Facility, see http://www.ncua.gov/Resources/CLF/Index.aspx and http://www.ncua.gov/Resources/CLF/CLF%20FAQs.pdf.

[86] P.L. 110-329, 122 Stat. 3574. See http://www.ncua.gov/Resources/Reports/NCUA2008-2009AnnualReport.pdf, p. 9.

[87] For discussions of the issues that required amending, see http://www.ncua.gov/newspublications/News/Newsletters/ NCUAReportFeb2011.pdf and Statement of Deborah Matz, chairman, National Credit Union Administration, "The State of the Credit Union Industry," p. 3, at http://www.ncua.gov/GenInfo/Members/Matz/speeches/ MatzState OfIndustryDec2010-Final.pdf, which was given in U.S. Congress, Senate Committee on Banking, Housing, and Urban Affairs, 111th Cong., 2nd sess., December 9, 2010.

[88] For more information about FASB, see http://www.fasb.org/home.

[89] See http://www.ncua.gov/Resources/Reports/plans-and-reports/2010/SupplementalCapital WhitePaper.pdf and http://www.ncua.gov/resources/RegulationsOpinionsLaws/ proposed_regs/Prompt%20Corrective%20Action%20Amended%20Definition%20of%20Post%20Mer ger%20Net%20Worth.pdf.

[90] The FDIC required its members to prepay deposit insurance assessments for three years to avoid having to borrow from Treasury, which was deemed less expensive on the industry.

[91] See http://www.ncua.gov/letters/2010/CU/10-CU-20.pdf and http://www.ncua.gov/GenInfo/BoardandAction/ DraftBoardActions/2010/Sep/Item1b10-0924.pdf.

[92] For definitions of these ratios as they apply to banking, see CRS Report R42744, *U.S. Implementation of the Basel Capital Regulatory Framework*, by Darryl E. Getter.

[93] See http://www.ncua.gov/letters/2010/CU/10-CU-17.pdf and http://www.ncua.gov/GenInfo/BoardandAction/reports/ 2010/BAB10-0916.pdf.

[94] See http://www.ncua.gov/resources

[95] See **Appendix A** for more information on the FDIC's TLGP and TAG programs.

[96] See http://www.ncua.gov/news/press_releases/2008/MA08-1016.htm.

[97] See http://www.ncua.gov/letters/2009/CU/Enclosure_2TemporaryCorporateShareGuarantee Program.pdf.

[98] See http://www.ncua.gov/resourcesand http://www.ncua.gov/ GenInfo/ BoardandAction /reports/2010/BAB10-0916.pdf.

INDEX

A

access, 3, 12, 47, 52, 59
accounting, viii, 2, 25, 46, 69, 71
accounting standards, 69
activity level, vii, 2, 4
adjustment, 36
agencies, x, 22, 26, 27, 29, 50
American Bar Association, 47
amortization, 33
appropriations, ix, 50
arbitrage, 25
assessment, 5, 26, 43, 62, 63, 64, 65, 66, 70, 74, 75
assets, 4, 5, 6, 7, 9, 10, 11, 12, 16, 17, 18, 19, 22, 23, 24, 25, 26, 27, 28, 29, 31, 34, 35, 37, 40, 41, 42, 43, 44, 45, 46, 47, 48, 52, 53, 57, 58, 59, 60, 63, 65, 73, 74, 75
authority(s), viii, ix, 21, 24, 26, 34, 35, 42, 49, 52, 59, 62, 63, 66, 68, 69, 72, 73, 74

B

balance sheet, 4, 18, 28, 33, 35, 40, 42, 44, 45, 46, 60, 61, 69
bank capital, viii, 9, 11, 18, 21, 22, 24, 30, 31
bank failure, ix, 5, 8, 29, 50, 51, 53, 59, 60, 61, 62, 65, 72, 74, 76
bank holding companies, viii, 22, 27, 28, 30, 36, 40, 41, 46, 47
bank loan-loss capacity, viii, 2
banking, vii, viii, 1, 2, 3, 4, 5, 7, 9, 12, 13, 16, 17, 19, 21, 22, 23, 24, 25, 27, 28, 29, 30, 33, 38, 40, 43, 44, 45, 46, 47, 48, 66, 71, 72, 73, 76
Banking Act of 1933, ix, 49, 52
banking industry, vii, viii, 1, 2, 3, 5, 7, 16
banking sector, 46
base, 34, 63, 64, 65, 66, 75
Basel Committee on Banking Supervision, viii, 21, 24, 34, 39, 42, 43, 46
basis points, 65, 66, 67, 70
Belgium, 42
bias, 56, 61, 62, 63, 66, 73
bonds, vii, 1, 2, 17, 36, 71
borrowers, 2, 3, 9, 11, 22, 23, 29, 45
business cycle, 3, 32, 35
business model, 16
businesses, 58, 67, 72
buyers, 37

C

Cambodia, 44
capitalization, vii, viii, 1, 2, 4, 18, 22, 24, 30, 31, 33, 38, 64
capitalization levels, vii, 1, 4, 22, 30, 31, 64
cash, 4, 26, 31, 37, 42, 44, 73

cash flow, 37, 73
central bank, viii, 21, 26, 34
certificates of deposit, 52
Chicago, 19
City, 19, 42, 44, 45
collateral, 23, 30, 57
commercial, vii, 1, 2, 3, 4, 12, 13, 31, 40, 41, 42, 54, 58, 59, 61, 66, 71
commercial bank, vii, 1, 3, 54
community, 5, 12, 17, 40, 47, 58
compensation, 29, 70
competition, 24
competitors, 24
compliance, 4, 11, 25, 26, 29, 32, 38, 43, 44, 46, 74
composition, 12, 31, 59
computation, 74
computer, 47
computing, 59
Conference Report, 43
Congress, viii, ix, 1, 18, 19, 21, 22, 26, 43, 45, 46, 47, 49, 50, 51, 52, 62, 68, 72, 73, 76
consensus, 24, 47
conservation, 34, 35
consolidation, 69
Constitution, 57
construction, 41, 61
consumers, 58, 72
correlation, 23, 73
cost, 2, 3, 29, 45, 73
covering, 66
credit rating, viii, 22, 26, 28, 33, 43
creditors, 4, 23, 24, 29, 58, 59, 71
creditworthiness, viii, 22, 26
crises, 30
customers, ix, 4, 23, 24, 29, 49, 51, 58, 59

D

Department of the Treasury, 18, 43
deposit accounts, 67, 71, 72, 75
depository banks, vii, 1, 2, 3, 16, 17
depository institutions, ix, x, 6, 12, 23, 27, 31, 46, 50, 51, 53, 61, 62, 63, 64, 67, 72, 73
deposits, vii, ix, x, 1, 2, 4, 12, 17, 19, 23, 37, 42, 44, 49, 50, 51, 52, 53, 57, 58, 59, 60, 64, 65, 66, 67, 69, 72, 73
directors, 70
distress, viii, 2, 11, 30, 36, 37, 73
distribution, 30, 35
Dodd-Frank Wall Street Reform and Consumer Protection Act, viii, 16, 18, 22, 26, 44, 51, 72

E

early warning, 45
earnings, viii, 2, 4, 7, 10, 16, 18, 25, 34, 35, 55, 66
economic activity, 3, 35
economic downturn, 3, 32, 56, 60, 73
economic growth, 37
economics, 42, 47, 74
education, 48
EESA, 52
emergency, 65, 68
Emergency Economic Stabilization Act, 52
employees, 71
environment, 11, 16
equity, 4, 7, 8, 11, 17, 24, 29, 31, 33, 34, 35, 36, 41, 44, 46, 56, 57, 59, 65, 68, 69, 70, 73, 74, 75
EU, 18
Europe, 41
European Central Bank, 18, 42
evidence, 16, 30
evolution, 53
examinations, 64
exercise, 66
expenditures, 68
expertise, 2
exposure, x, 16, 32, 44, 45, 50

F

faith, 72
Fannie Mae, vii, 1, 2, 12, 45, 73, 74
FDIC, ix, x, 4, 5, 6, 7, 8, 9, 10, 13, 14, 15, 16, 17, 18, 19, 46, 49, 50, 51, 52, 53, 54, 55, 58, 59, 60, 61, 62, 63, 64, 65, 66, 67, 70, 71, 72, 73, 74, 75, 76
federal agency, ix, 26, 50, 54
federal credit unions, ix, 50, 54
federal funds, 42, 59
federal government, 13
Federal Register, 18, 43, 75
Federal Reserve, 18, 19, 30, 36, 38, 41, 42, 43, 44, 45, 46, 47, 48, 54, 68, 72
Federal Reserve Board, 18, 19
financial condition, vii, 1, 3, 5, 25, 39, 40
financial crisis, vii, 1, 5, 6, 16, 22, 25, 26, 30, 34, 42, 51
financial distress, 3, 6, 51, 53
financial instability, 30
financial institutions, ix, 5, 23, 24, 34, 37, 39, 40, 45, 49, 53, 62, 63, 65, 67, 72, 73
financial markets, 12, 13, 37, 38, 42
financial risks, vii, ix, 1, 4, 22, 26, 29, 30, 32, 36
financial shocks, viii, 21
financial stability, 44
financial system, ix, 23, 30, 31, 35, 47, 49, 51
flexibility, 69
flight, 13
fluctuations, 3, 16, 19, 59
foreclosure, 18
France, 42
fraud, 71
Freddie Mac, vii, 1, 2, 12, 45, 73, 74
funding, viii, 2, 3, 12, 13, 16, 17, 23, 29, 30, 34, 37, 38, 40, 46, 47, 58, 64, 65, 66, 68, 71
funds, x, 2, 4, 11, 12, 17, 19, 23, 37, 50, 51, 52, 53, 54, 58, 59, 60, 61, 62, 65, 68, 71, 72

G

GDP, 41
Germany, 18, 42
Glass-Steagall Act, ix, 17, 50, 52
global recession, 41
government securities, 32, 37, 55
governments, 17, 24
Gramm-Leach-Bliley Act, 17
Greece, 46
growth, 7, 11, 13, 16, 17, 35
growth rate, 11, 13, 16
GSA, 17
guidance, 29, 40, 41, 43, 47
guidelines, 28
guiding principles, 47

H

health, 51
history, 18
holding company, 27
home value, 61
House, 73, 74, 76
House of Representatives, 74, 76
housing, 26, 45
hybrid, 28

I

ideal, 3
illiquid asset, 37
income, 3, 6, 7, 8, 10, 12, 16, 17, 18, 25, 55, 59
individuals, 3, 75
industry, vii, viii, 1, 2, 4, 5, 6, 7, 8, 10, 11, 16, 61, 66, 75, 76
industry consolidation, 5
institutions, vii, viii, ix, x, 1, 2, 3, 4, 5, 6, 7, 9, 12, 16, 17, 22, 23, 24, 25, 27, 28, 30, 37, 40, 41, 42, 43, 44, 45, 48, 49, 50, 51, 54, 55, 59, 60, 62, 63, 64, 65, 66, 67, 72, 73, 75
interest margins, 12, 13, 16

investment(s), 29, 32, 53, 57, 68, 70, 71, 73
investors, 16, 17, 23, 26, 29
issues, vii, x, 2, 19, 28, 44, 50, 76
Italy, 42

J

Japan, 42

L

laws, 72
LBA, 17
lead, viii, 21, 24, 54
lending, vii, viii, ix, 1, 2, 3, 4, 5, 7, 11, 12, 13, 16, 17, 22, 23, 25, 26, 30, 32, 33, 35, 38, 40, 41, 44, 47, 49, 50, 59, 63, 66
lending patterns, viii, 2, 16
light, 28, 30, 42, 63
liquid assets, 31, 37, 38, 59
liquidate, 37, 69, 74
liquidity, x, 2, 3, 23, 29, 31, 33, 36, 37, 38, 47, 50, 51, 54, 57, 59, 64, 66, 68, 72, 73
liquidity ratio, 34, 38, 73
loan defaults, viii, 2, 4, 8, 21, 24, 25, 32, 37, 40, 61, 66
loan guarantees, 36
loans, vii, viii, 1, 2, 3, 4, 9, 10, 11, 12, 13, 16, 18, 23, 28, 29, 30, 31, 32, 33, 36, 37, 38, 41, 42, 53, 58, 59, 60, 69, 73
local government, 17
long-term customer, 42
low risk, 31

M

magnitude, 11, 63, 64
management, 40, 41, 46, 70
market discipline, 46
media, 17, 42, 74
medicine, 47
membership, 61
mergers, 69
methodology, 22, 29, 46
models, 48, 75
modifications, viii, 21, 27, 38, 65
money markets, 12, 19, 42
mortgage-backed securities, 57

N

National Credit Union Administration (NCUA), ix, 50, 51, 54
National Credit Union Share Insurance Fund (NCUSIF), ix, 50, 51
Netherlands, 42
non-OECD, 32
NPR, 28, 29, 33, 44, 63

O

OECD, 32, 46
officials, 38
operations, 55
opportunities, 16
opt out, 67
optimism, 30
oversight, x, 50
ownership, 52, 68

P

parents, 27
participants, 23, 42
payroll, 12, 67, 72
PCA, 47
penalties, 38, 55
permission, 45
pessimism, 23
pharmacology, 47
policy, 34
portfolio, ix, 22, 24, 26, 29, 31, 36, 41, 58, 59
portfolio capital, 31
present value, 59
President, 62
private sector, 32
profit, 3, 53

profitability, vii, viii, 1, 2, 3, 5, 7, 8, 10, 11, 13, 16, 17, 38, 42, 62, 73
profitability ratios, 16
profitability trends, viii, 2, 17
propagation, 3

R

rate of return, 2
RE, 40
real estate, 12, 23, 40, 41, 61
recession, 5, 8, 11, 12, 16, 23, 25, 40, 61, 74
recommendations, 38
recovery, vii, 1, 30, 32
reform(s), viii, 16, 18, 21, 22, 26, 33, 43, 44, 51, 52, 62, 72, 74
regulations, 3, 17, 18, 25, 26, 44, 46, 72, 75
regulatory agencies, 38, 43
regulatory framework, viii, 21, 24, 26
regulatory requirements, 22, 23
reimburse, 51, 59, 60
relationship banking, 12
requirements, viii, 5, 9, 12, 13, 16, 18, 21, 22, 24, 25, 26, 27, 28, 29, 30, 32, 33, 38, 40, 41, 44, 46, 48, 58, 70
reserves, x, 4, 6, 11, 22, 23, 24, 31, 37, 38, 42, 50, 53, 55, 59, 62
resilience, 37
resolution, 51, 58, 59, 73, 74
resources, 34, 44, 74, 75, 76, 77
response, 19, 25, 26, 65
restoration, 53, 56, 65
restrictions, 38, 61, 62, 70
retail, 12, 51, 53, 71
retained earnings, 4, 24, 34
retirement, 52, 54, 71, 72
revenue, viii, ix, 2, 6, 12, 42, 49
rights, 34
risk(s), vii, ix, x, 1, 3, 4, 6, 9, 10, 11, 12, 16, 17, 18, 19, 22, 23, 24, 25, 26, 27, 28, 29, 30, 31, 32, 33, 35, 36, 37, 38, 40, 41, 42, 43, 44, 45, 46, 50, 52, 59, 60, 62, 63, 64, 65, 70, 73, 74, 75
risk assessment, 17
risk management, 41
risk profile, 63
rules, 18, 22, 24, 25, 26, 44, 74

S

safety, 3, 13, 23, 24, 29, 30, 58, 70, 74
savings, 4, 5, 43, 52, 58, 67, 71
savings account, 52, 71
SCAP, 41, 48
scarcity, 37
security(s), vii, viii, 1, 2, 4, 13, 16, 17, 22, 23, 25, 26, 28, 31, 32, 36, 37, 38, 42, 43, 44, 45, 46, 71
self-employed, 71
sellers, 37
Senate, 18, 19, 43, 73, 76
sensitivity, 46
services, vii, 1, 2, 12, 16, 51, 53, 70, 72
shareholders, 8, 24, 29
shortage, 38
short-term interest rate, 3, 19, 58
showing, 10
signs, 10, 16
single cap, 70
Spain, 42, 45
speculation, 3, 51
speech, 45, 47, 48
Spring, 19, 71
stability, 16, 35
state(s), vii, 1, 2, 17, 41, 42, 69, 71, 72
stock, 28, 37, 42, 44
stress, 25, 29, 30, 35, 37, 39, 40, 41, 45, 48
stress test, 25, 29, 30, 39, 40, 41, 45, 48
stress testing, 25, 29, 30, 40, 41, 45, 48
structure, 65, 74
supervision, 39, 42, 45
Sweden, 42
Switzerland, 42, 44, 45, 46, 48
systemic risk, 22, 23, 25, 30, 38, 44, 47, 60

T

taxpayers, 60, 61
territory, 16

testing, 25, 40, 47
theft, 71
threshold level, 4, 24, 32
thrifts, 72
total costs, 76
trade, 3
trade-off, 3
transactions, 2, 3, 12, 16
transparency, 34
Treasury, 38, 43, 44, 61, 62, 66, 68, 69, 71, 72, 76
treaties, viii, 21
treatment, 25

U

U.S. Department of the Treasury, 43, 45
U.S. economy, 16
U.S. Treasury, 31, 38, 44, 51, 61, 62, 66, 68, 69
underwriting, 12, 17, 19, 28, 40, 45, 46, 63, 64
unemployment rate, 10, 41
uninsured, 52, 70, 71, 72
unions, ix, 2, 50, 51, 53, 54, 55, 57, 58, 60, 61, 68, 69, 70, 71, 72, 73, 74
United, viii, ix, 17, 22, 24, 25, 26, 27, 31, 42, 44, 49, 50, 57, 67
United Kingdom, 42
United States, viii, ix, 17, 22, 24, 25, 26, 27, 31, 42, 44, 49, 50, 67

V

variables, 64
vehicles, 73
volatility, 16
vulnerability, 3, 25, 30

W

Washington, 17, 18, 19, 46, 47, 73
wholesale, 53
workers, 61